Why Am I on This Planet?

Todd M. Oberlander

VANTAGE PRESS
New York

FIRST EDITION

Published by Vantage Press, Inc.
516 West 34th Street, New York, New York 10001

Manufactured in the United States of America
ISBN: 0-533-12786- 6

Library of Congress Catalog Card No.: 98-90367

0 9 8 7 6 5 4 3 2 1

I would like to thank you, Lord, for giving me the inspiration to write this book. Thank you for giving me the encouragement and support I needed during those times when I felt this book was much too great a task for me to write. All those times you woke me up in the middle of the night to give me topics to write about have certainly been a blessing to me. It also turned out to be a great time for me to praise you and I truly enjoyed your presence. I would also like to thank my wife for encouraging me to pursue my dreams in life. Without their help I would not be where I am today.

This book is dedicated to the loving memory of Pastor David and Sandy Hensley, two of the most wonderful people I have ever had the privilege of meeting. They spread their love around the Dayton and Middletown, Ohio, area. They weren't afraid to hold a mirror in front of your face so you could see yourself for who you really were. Then they would nurture you with love and care, and direct you in the ways of our Heavenly Father. I feel very fortunate to have had them as my youth pastors and friends. I'm sure they were a blessing to all the lives they touched.

Love Always,
Todd

P.S. Thanks, Sleepy Ray, for allowing me to include the lyrics of your song in my book. If I could choose only one word to describe your music, that word would be "cool."

Contents

Foreword

Most people are just ordinary folks like Todd and myself. Growing up in rural South Dakota, we could not have been more average if we had tried. If there was an award for the "most likely to be lost in obscurity," we would have tied. But something terrific happened to us and our lives are now more fulfilling than anyone could have imagined.

Picture a row of hammers at the hardware store. One does not differ from another much at all. In fact, their differences are very minute until you compare them to the craftsmen that will eventually use them. Like a hammer destined for use by both skilled and unskilled craftsmen, the true differences between people are revealed in the world views that guide them. I'd rather be an average hammer in the hands of a Jewish carpenter than a state-of-the-art reactive neodymium carbon fiber hammer being wielded by a madman.

Taking sole control of our lives is comparable to a hammer attempting to build a house by itself. The result is a mess suitable only for burning. Many of us have battled the decision of WHO is controlling our lives. Christ can take the mess from our feeble attempt at constructing our lives and rebuild it properly, but only if He is asked and only if everything is given over to Him. It is often difficult to understand how another day in the life of an average person could possibly fit into God's great plan. We may feel like a hammer as we pound away at our daily tasks, not realizing that God is working in our lives in ways we cannot comprehend. Like a hammer in the carpenter's hands, we are unaware of what God does while we are not looking, or seeing.

In his autobiography, *Just As I Am*, the renowned evangelist Billy Graham recounts his search for God's purpose. Days turned into weeks and then into years, and God was using Mr. Graham even though he was unaware. He will use you, too.

Being part of a generation that holds education in such high regard, it baffles me that there are only a few who guard against spiritual ignorance. This generation is not teaching the concepts of right and wrong. What was black and white is now relegated to shades of gray in the spirit of accommodation. Values have become subjective. Absolutes are dying.

We feel an emptiness created by spiritual bankruptcy but don't recognize its origin; we unconsciously fill the void with unhealthy and destructive behavior. Some people are aware enough to look for answers and that is where this book is important. Our society spends too much time, money, and energy dealing with the effects of unsuccessful spiritual searches, but we blatantly refuse the answer which has already been offered and paid in full.

The thirst for hope is tremendous, yet so many people are never able to quench it. Too many of God's children become browbeaten and brainwashed—and reject hope when it is offered.

Hope is here, right now. The battle has been won and the victory is ours to claim. Nothing can separate us from a victorious life in Christ except our own rejection of it. God's purpose may not always be clear, but it will become so in time. The most important thing is our daily walk with Christ. The rest will be done when we aren't looking. This is a book full of truths, helpful at any age or stage in our walks with Christ. Read them, guard them, share them, delight in them. They are yours by the grace of God.

—Jim D. Holdahl

Introduction

Does anyone have an answer yet? Why are we on this planet? This is a question that has crossed my mind many times in life. Why do so many things in life happen differently from the way we plan for them to happen? Why should we plan anything? Why should we worry about life? Why should we set our goals and try so hard to achieve them within a certain time frame? Why should we put so much pressure on ourselves? One of man's basic instincts is to provide for his family, but sometimes we try too hard to accomplish our goals. We get caught up in the fast-paced society of today where we can have everything we want right now.

One day I found the secret to a happier, more contented life. As many people do, I went through the first stages of my life pondering what life is really about. I truly know in my heart that I have found the answer to my question. I discovered the answer one day when I asked Jesus Christ to come into my heart, forgive me of my sins, and be the Lord of my life. Something happened inside me when I had the faith to believe that Jesus Christ is really the Son of God, and that he really did come to Earth to sacrifice his life for our sins, so that we might be able to enter God's kingdom of heaven. The trick was having the faith to believe. That is where the breakthrough occurs.

One of my main prayers throughout the course of my life is that God would work his will in my life. When you say a prayer like this, you know that anything is bound to happen. I was afraid that God might ask me to be a missionary to a country where people lived in tents and rode elephants for transportation. Hey, wait a minute . . . God isn't going to force us to do anything we don't desire . . . or is he? And, what is so bad about riding an elephant as long as God is with you? How many people do you know who are still paying their mortgage on their tent? Sometimes we get so caught up in providing for ourselves, we forget that God is our provider. We need to learn when to put our goals on the back burner and tune in to what God wants us to do with our lives. This book is about how I planned my life, how God planned my life, and the things he has taught me along the way.

One

Life Is a Choice

Life is nothing but a continuous decision-making process from start to finish. Through the decisions we make in life, we hold the power to make our dreams come true, or to cause the world around us to topple over and crush us. Many of the choices we make in life usually affect more of our life than we realize. By tapping into God when we face a decision, we have the power to see what can transpire as a result of our decisions. God will reveal to us the consequences that can take place from any decision we are about to make. This can ultimately lead us to the correct decision to make regarding any circumstance. Through God's help, we have the power to make all the choices that are right for our lives, but the first choice we must make is to include God in our decision-making process.

Many people don't realize just how much the choices they make reflect their lives and the lives of those around them. We can choose to be responsible in our decision-making, or we can take the lazy way out. It is all too easy to disregard many of the consequences of the choices we make, or fail to even acknowledge that any consequences exist. We go on as if we are just going through another daily routine. As the day passes, we can easily accept the views of negativity that this world throws at us.

We could choose to believe that our life is just a bunch of years that are strung together, with each year having three hun-

1

dred and sixty-five days of those average daily routines. We could choose to believe that each day of our life is just another ship sailing by. We could choose to believe that there is no meaning to life other than our own immediate concerns. We could choose to believe that there is no way we could make a difference in the lives of the people around us. We could choose to believe that the things spoken of in the Bible are not true, or that maybe they are true and they are just not attainable. We could choose to believe that the Bible only applies to people who lived thousands of years ago, and that it doesn't apply to life in today's world. We could choose to believe that the Bible was written by a drunken bunch of bums, whose sole purpose was to confuse the rest of the world for eternity (all right, maybe that one is stretching it a bit).

On the other hand, we could choose to have faith and believe that everything that the Bible speaks of is attainable because, after all, the Bible is God's word to man. When honorable people give you their word, you know that they aren't lying. How much more honorable can you get than God himself? Everything that God's word says is the truth, and the keys to life are all inside, just waiting for us to discover them. All it takes is a little bit of positive attitude instead of negative. All it takes is faith, and faith is a choice that we make to believe in the Bible or the fact that God even exists. The choice to believe in God and the Bible is a choice that holds the largest determining factor of how our life will play out. If we choose to believe in God, and include him in our daily decision process, we hold the answer to life in the palms of our hands. But first, we must choose to apply God and the Bible to our life. We must choose to believe and act upon what we believe.

One example of how our choices can affect the world around us is the approach that my wife and I take to our marriage. After we were married, many people said to us, "Just wait, in a few years your marriage flame will burn out and everything will get old real fast." I can't recall how many people said that to us before we got married. It seemed as if everyone was being negative about marriage. They told us that after our first six months together, we would start getting tired of being around each other. Six months passed and they all said to give it another six months. Then two years passed and they were all saying it would happen any day now. Three years, and four years passed, and they are all saying the same doom and gloom story. We were in Williamsburg, Virginia, one year and a lady asked my wife if we were on our honeymoon. You should have seen how surprised she was when she found out we were celebrating our fifth anniversary. Six years passed, seven years, and eight years, and now we are approaching our ninth year of marriage and we still act like a couple of lovebirds. I wonder if all those people who sang the old doom and gloom story are wondering what is wrong with us or why we aren't changing? It's really very simple. When my wife and I married, we made an agreement to never treat each other like an old worn-out pair of gym shoes. We both agreed to do whatever it takes to keep the flame burning inside our marriage. So far we have accomplished our goal and it gets easier as each day passes. It wasn't always easy. Many times the old selfish human nature kicked in and we weren't considering each other's thoughts or feelings. But when reality hit us, we remembered that we had made a commitment to each other. We talked out our problems, forgave each other, called it a learning experience, and moved on.

One of the things we still do is go out for an evening and paint the town red just as when we were dating. So if you get out of bed one day and look out your window and see red cars, red houses, red trees, and red bushes, you will know that my wife and I were passing through your neighborhood the night before. As we focus on what God wants out of us, it helps us to keep our marriage in the right perspective. It isn't what you get out of marriage that makes it work; it's what you put into your marriage. I am extremely thankful for the love that makes our marriage tick. That love that is beyond all measure. The love that God puts inside of us for each other. As long as God is the center of our marriage, we will always have that special something that makes our marriage wonderful. We would never have had as great a marriage as we do now if we had not made the choice to keep God the center of our marriage, or the choice to be committed to keeping the spice in our marriage.

I happened across another example of choices we make in life that affect the world around us one day as I was watching television. A popular news and information program was doing a story on a lady who had been on a recent talk show. This talk show was definitely your typical talk show format. They had this lady set up real good. They had the lady express her personal beliefs against placing children in a day-care center. The people who ran the talk show purposely invited a bunch of people who were strongly in favor of day-care centers. They love to try to make people squirm. This is their distorted view of entertainment. The lady stated many very good reasons as to why she was against day care, and how the choice to put children in most day-care centers can have a negative impact on a child and can drastically change the way a child learns and grows. Of course, all the women in the audience who were in favor of day-care centers took this lady's comments too personally, as if she were saying their children were terrible kids. They began lashing out at her, saying things such as, "How dare you judge the decisions we make!" The lady was trying to show them how the decisions they make can affect their children's lives. The audience continued to tear into her until she finally drove home her point. She asked the audience this question: "Suppose you had the opportunity to choose. Disregard your personal beliefs concerning your present situation, and the financial aspect of considering your extra income as necessary. If the power had been totally yours to choose during your own childhood, how many of you in the audience would choose to have been raised in a day-care center rather than in your own home?" Not one person in the audience raised a hand or had a reply. The point she went on to make is that as we look at things through a different perspective, starting at the results and working back to the point where the decision is made, it makes it easier for us to make better decisions for ourselves and our children.

That is precisely what God does when we include him in our decision-making process. As we take our situation to him, He shows us a bigger picture. We now can see the whole forest instead of just the trees around us. When we see the big picture, we see the direction we should be heading. This is what helps us make the correct decision for where we are today. If we become consciously aware of the fact that every day we can make a choice about something in our lives, whether it is how we choose to react to other people around us or whatever the case, we can realize that we have more control over our outlook on life and the direction our life is headed than we may think we have.

We can choose to attempt this life on our own, or we can choose to walk through this life with the help of our Heavenly Father. If we can establish a true relationship with God, built on love and trust in God, we can talk with God and share our concerns and struggles in life. We then can receive from God the support and encouragement that we all need as individuals. Once we come to know God as he truly is, the bond that occurs between us and God is a bond so strong that virtually nothing can break it. By developing such a relationship as this with our Heavenly Father, we are in effect taking control of our lives and locking in our eternal destiny to be directed towards God.

God has a specific purpose for the life of each one of us. But, God is also a gentleman. He allows us to choose whether we will or will not follow after his will for our life. God wants to know if we are willing to seek his plan for our lives, even if it involves some sacrifice. Are we willing enough to make the decision to seek after God's will for our lives? Are we willing enough to allow God to work in our lives and transform us into who he wants us to be? Situations can change, people can change, forgiveness can take place, but in order for any change to take place, it must first start inside each of us individually. The situation will not change itself. Nobody else is going to change the situation for us. God wants us to take our situation to him so that he can work with us to change our attitudes toward our situations. That is where change begins to take place. That is where forgiveness begins to take place. That is where growth as an individual occurs. Life is a choice, and the choice is ours to make. The more we cast our cares upon God, the more we are able to operate in love and forgiveness, that's all the more we will grow in our knowledge of what life is really about. That is just how much closer we are to discovering why we are on this planet and what our purpose is in life.

So many times in life we look for someone to blame for why our life has turned out the way it has. Many people wonder if there really is a God or how God could allow certain things to happen to them. Other people choose to cast the blame for everything upon God, thinking that if there truly was a God, he never would have allowed many of those things to happen. That is one of the biggest mistakes people make. It's not God's fault that our life has taken the course that it has. We bring many things upon ourselves just by the choices we make every day in life.

Our lives are also affected by choices that other people have made for us. For example, parents make many choices when their children are young, which have a direct impact upon how a child's life turns out. God gave us a way of salvation through Jesus Christ, but he left the choice up to us as to whether or not we will serve him. If God wanted to save us all from a destiny of eternal damnation, he could do it in a heartbeat. But God, being the loving father that he is, allowed us to choose whether or not we want to serve him. God gave us the choice to serve him or to serve the devil. We are all serving one or the other, whether we want to or not. God also gave us the key to salvation through Jesus Christ his Son. He sent Jesus into this world to live a life of perfection and to sacrifice his life for all of the sins of man by dying on the cross. When Jesus did this, he became the perfect sacrifice for our sins so that we might obtain our salvation through accepting Jesus Christ as our Savior from sin. Then God gave us an instruction manual to help us through life and to answer all of our questions about life. God gave us the keys to the car and the instruction manual on how to drive. Then he gave us the choice of two separate roads to drive on. One road leads to Heaven and the other road leads to Hell. He lets us choose which road we want to take, and each road ends at the stopping point of our soul's eternal destination.

We are all driving somewhere in life. The question is, where do you want to be when the road in your life ends? If you are driving down the wrong road in life, just turn around and start driving down the right road, which is the road to salvation. You will never regret the choice you made, especially when this life is over and your reward is Heaven.

God has a will or a purpose for every person in this world. It is up to us to find out what God's will is and make the choice to pursue God's will for our life. How do we know what God's will is for our life? How do we know we are not following our own selfish desires? We may not know what God's will is for us, but if we search our own hearts, we will know whether the decision we are making is correct or not, based on the feelings we display in our heart. If our decision is motivated by bad feelings, then it is the wrong decision to make.

Even though we may not know what God's will is, we can

make our decisions by searching our hearts and eliminating the decisions motivated by bad feelings. Then, all we have left are the right decisions to make. You will know in your heart when you have made the right decision because you will have a good feeling in your heart about that decision. You will be doing the right thing for the right reason. The main thing to keep in mind is that we must make our decisions based on what God wants us to do. That may not always be something that we desire. Don't get me wrong. Everyone deserves to obtain the finer things in life and it is good to reward ourselves. We just need to be careful not to get caught up in our own greed or we will be heading down the wrong road.

Romans 4:23–25, 5:1, 2

Now it was not written for his sake alone, that it was imputed to him; But for us also, to whom it shall be imputed, if we believe on him that raised up Jesus our Lord from the dead; Who was delivered for our offences, and was raised again for our justification. Therefore being justified by faith, we have peace with God through our Lord Jesus Christ: By whom also we have access by faith into this grace wherein we stand, and rejoice in hope of the glory of God.

2 Corinthians 5:7

For we walk by faith, not by sight:

Galatians 2:16–20

Knowing that a man is not justified by the works of the law, but by the faith of Jesus Christ, even we have believed in Jesus Christ, that we might be justified by the faith of Christ, and not by the works of the law: for by the works of the law shall no flesh be justified. But if, while we seek to be justified by

8

Christ, we ourselves also are found sinners, is therefore Christ the minister of sin? God forbid. For if I build again the things which I destroyed, I make myself a transgressor. For I through the law am dead to the law, that I might live unto God. I am crucified with Christ: nevertheless I live; yet not I, but Christ liveth in me: and the life which I now live in the flesh I live by the faith of the Son of God, who loved me, and gave himself for me.

Galatians 3:11

But that no man is justified by the law in the sight of God, it is evident; for, The just shall live by faith.

Ephesians 2:8, 9

For by grace are ye saved through faith; and that not of yourselves: it is the gift of God: Not of works, lest any man should boast.

Hebrews 11:1–6

Now faith is the substance of things hoped for, the evidence of things not seen. For by it the elders obtained a good report. Through faith we understand that the worlds were framed by the word of God, so that things which are seen were not made of things which do appear. By faith Abel offered unto God a more excellent sacrifice than Cain, by which he obtained witness that he was righteous, God testifying of his gifts: and by it he being dead yet speaketh. By faith Enoch was translated that he should not see death; and was not found, because God had translated him: for before his translation he had this testimony, that he pleased God. But without faith it is impossible to please him: for he that cometh to God must believe that he is, and that he is a rewarder of them that diligently seek him.

9

Psalms 34:8

O taste and see that the Lord is good: blessed is the man that trusteth in him.

Matthew 17:20

And Jesus said unto them, Because of your unbelief: for verily I say unto you, If ye have faith as a grain of mustard seed, ye shall say unto this mountain, Remove hence to yonder place; and it shall remove; and nothing shall be impossible unto you.

1 John 5:11–15

And this is the record, that God hath given to us eternal life, and this life is in his Son. He that hath the Son hath life; and he that hath not the Son of God hath not life. These things have I written unto you that believe on the name of the Son of God; that ye may know that ye have eternal life, and that ye may believe on the name of the Son of God. And this is the confidence that we have in him, that, if we ask any thing according to his will, he heareth us: And if we know that he heareth us, whatsoever we ask, we know that we have the petitions that we desired of him.

Two
Letting God Have Control

Sometimes life seems to be like watching a movie, except you can use a remote control to make decisions for the main character. Many times we like to experiment. We push too many buttons and make a mess of everything. God wants us to be in control of our lives, but sometimes when we don't know what to do, we need to turn the controls over to him and let him work through us.

Back in my senior year of high school, I joined the track team. It was fun being able to goof off with my friends on the team. We all got to know each other a little better during that time. One day, after practice, there were about six of us in the locker room kidding around as we usually did, and something happened that I was not prepared for. There was a lull in the conversation and it seemed everyone was waiting for someone to say something. Then, one of the guys who had seemed to have something bothering him spoke up. "Hey, Todd," he said. "How come you are always so happy all of the time? I have never seen you in a bad mood," he continued. "You are always so happy. Why?" At this point everyone was looking at me, waiting for an answer.

This had caught me totally off guard. It was at a time in my life when I tried to be a Christian, but I didn't know how to control my temptations. I had a lot of problems in my walk with God and was afraid to tell them about Christ because of

11

what their reaction might be. I didn't want to be rejected by them because for once in my life it seemed as if I was one of the gang. My heart felt an urge to say something about how happy my life became when I accepted Christ as my Savior, but the pressure of the moment was too much for me, so I told them I just tried to have a positive outlook on life. I felt terrible. Not only had I let God down, but I had also let my friends down.

At that time our senior year was almost over and this was one of the last times we would see each other. After graduation, people generally don't get together with a lot of their high school friends anymore. There was really nothing for me to lose in this situation and to this day I wish I had told them about Christ. One of my prayers is that someday someone will have more courage than I did and will witness to them. I also pray that they will be receptive to God's word and will accept Christ into their lives.

This was a time when I should have given the controls to God and said what he wanted me to say, but I was too busy playing around with my Christianity and pushing all of the wrong buttons on my remote control. When we become Christians, not only can we enjoy the peace and happiness of life, we also have a mandate to act and respond the way a Christian should. We must develop the discipline it takes to operate our remote control responsibly.

Just as there are times when we have the remote control and can make choices, there are also times when God has the remote control and is helping us make the right choices without our ever being aware of the difference. One day my wife was teasing with me and singing a song that she knew I didn't care for. I wanted to listen to some music, but not that particular song and she knew it. I turned on our stereo system and started playing some music. My wife started singing louder. I proceeded to crank up the volume so I couldn't hear her any more. She picked up the remote control and turned the volume down and continued singing. Once again, I blasted the volume to drown her out and she followed by lowering the volume with the remote. I finally got my hands on the remote control so she couldn't turn the volume down. Here I thought I would fix her by blasting the volume when I found she also had control of the stereo with another remote. Sometimes we think we are in control, but we don't realize that someone else may also be in control. Sometimes we think we are in control when it is God who is really in control.

When I graduated from high school, I was fed up with education. My desire was to never touch another book. I wanted to experience life on my own, so I moved from Dayton, Ohio, to South Dakota, where most of my family was. I also didn't have any desire to return to Dayton. It was great just to be able to provide a life for myself. I had my youth, my freedom, and not a worry in the world. It didn't take long for me to learn what the real world was like. Life was a little rougher than it seemed it would be. I began to desire more out of life than I had achieved.

After one year passed, I decided to attend college. I wasn't even sure why I was going to college. I just wanted to get a feel for what college would be like. My major was drafting technology. Drawing was always one of my better talents, so it seemed natural that drafting would be easy for me. Another positive factor was that drafting only required attaining an associate degree. When the first semester began, I enjoyed my classes so much that I decided to stick it out for two years and see what happened. After I finished college, I ended up moving back to Dayton.

Life sure is strange sometimes. Somehow, God changed my desires so he would be able to accomplish his will for my life. After all, my main prayer was for God's will to be done in my life. So, why did I get an education and move back to Dayton? These were two things that I swore I would never do. I didn't know it at the time, but God wanted me to be a witness to some of the employees at the various engineering firms I would work for and also to some of my old high school buddies. My future wife also lived in Dayton. When you look at the results, following God's will for my life wasn't so bad after all. I have made some new friends and restored some old friendships. Most of all God's direction has given me a wonderful life filled with happiness and that is what counts the most.

One thing that this experience taught me was to never say I would never do something. If my desire is for God's will to be done in my life, it is essential for me to subject myself to whatever he might want from me. By choosing God's will for my life, I must also choose to forfeit the right to do things my way. I must let God have total control over my life. One of the great things about God is that as I am giving my life to God, he is giving back to me everything that I desire of my heart. I don't even have to be selfish because God gives me all the desires of my heart. This endless loop of giving back and forth continues throughout the course of our lives, but as I mentioned previously, the choice always begins with us. This choice is not always easy because we have to deal with our inner desire to do things our way. But when we experience that God's way is ultimately the better way, the choice becomes easier the next time because we have experienced the goodness that God has for us.

Ecclesiastes 8:5–7

Who so keepeth the commandment shall feel no evil thing: and a wise man's heart discerneth both time and judgment. Because to every purpose there is time and judgment, therefore the misery of man is great upon him. For he knoweth not that which shall be: for who can tell him when it shall be?

1 Peter 3:15–17

But sanctify the Lord God in your hearts: and be ready always to give an answer to every man that asketh you a reason of the hope that is in you with meekness and fear: having a good conscience; that, whereas they speak evil of you, as of evildoers, they may be ashamed that falsely accuse your good conversation in Christ. For it is better, if the will of God be so, that ye suffer for well doing, than for evil doing.

Psalms 16:11

Thou wilt shew me the path of life; in thy presence is fullness of joy; at thy right hand there are pleasures for evermore.

Psalms 37:4

Delight thyself also in the Lord; and he shall give thee the desires of thine heart.

Proverbs 16:9

A man's heart diviseth his way: but the Lord directeth his steps.

Lord, even though we are only human and are bound to fail at times, please grant us the wisdom and courage we need in order to keep living our lives for you. Help us to keep reading our Bibles so that when the time comes for us to witness to others, your word will be written on the tables of our hearts. Help us to know your voice and to listen when we hear you telling us to do something. Help us to be the faithful servants that you want us to be. Help us to give you the controls when you ask for them so that we will not push all of the wrong buttons.

Faith before Logic

I first accepted Christ as my Savior when I was a young boy. I was so young I don't remember what my age was at the time. When I started school, I was picked on by some of the other kids because I was the smallest kid in the class. And everyone also had to put up with the typical class bully who had been held back a few grades. It was during this time my dad started driving for a trucking company. He spent his first five years working the longer routes across the United States and we were lucky to see him one week out of the year. During those five years, whenever I needed advice from a father, I learned to listen to what God was quietly telling me on the inside. Every time I followed God's directions, my problems would always work out no matter how big they seemed. It was easy for my faith in God to grow tremendously during those years because children always remember and are always loyal to someone who gives great advice and is never wrong.

Now, I am older and have a lot more experience in life. At times my faith level seems greater now than it was then, and other times it seems like nothing when I compare it to my childhood. There are times when I can come up with a solution to solve my problems, but my solution may not be God's solution. I'm sure my faith level has grown a lot since I was a boy, but sometimes it seems I have to try three times harder to get the same results. It was easier for me as a child because of my innocence. As a child, I didn't know what to do. I didn't have any solutions of my own. When I needed a solution to a problem, I would ask God what I should do. God would tell me what to do and I would do it. It sure sounds simple enough, doesn't it? One of the things I am working harder at is to remember that I am trying to follow God's will, not Todd's will. I carry a picture in my wallet of myself when I was a boy to always remind myself that God is in control and all I have to do is listen to his voice and follow his directions. Nevertheless, there are always those times where the simplest little things seem to jump out at me and test my faith.

One of those simple little things is logic. There have been too many times in life when logic has told me what was about to happen. I would look at a given situation and figure out how to handle my problem in a logical manner. The problem is that life does not follow a logical course. Anything can happen to anyone at any given moment. Let's look at our bills, for example.

Most people have experienced having more bills at the end of the month than they have money to pay those bills. So, what do we do about it? We take a good look at our income and plan a way to save money each month. Then, we try to pay off our debt over the next couple of months. We have created a logical way to solve our problem. A couple of months later, the washer is on the blink, a few other things have happened, and we find ourselves in the same situation as we were in the past. One thing after another happens and we find ourselves worrying about how we will pay our bills each month.

The first time this happened to me, I was a basket case. I found myself worrying about my bills almost every day for about eight months before finally getting them under control. My problem slowly started eating away at the inside of me. Eventually, my problem escalated to the point where it consumed me and controlled my thoughts, my actions, and my life. I wasn't able to relax and enjoy life until my bills were under control.

I looked back at the events that had taken place and began to wonder what made me worry so much. My problem was that I looked at my situation too logically and thought it would never be possible for me to work my way out of it. That is what caused all of my worrying. Eight months of my life were just wasted because I had allowed this situation to make me miserable. What was even worse was that when the Charles Dickens classic *A Christmas Carol* was shown on television, I began to see that my actions had been similar to the actions of Ebenezer Scrooge. *Lord, help me to change,* I thought. Whoever this person was that I had become certainly was not my normal self and I no longer desired to act as I had in the past.

A couple of years later, I would find myself in a situation that would be five times as bad as the previous experience. Once again I began to react in the same manner as before. I started becoming bitter and angry. As stubborn as I was, I didn't want to admit that anything was bothering me. God began to show me that my problems were once again controlling my actions. It was then I decided not to let this happen anymore. Instead, I prayed that God would grant me the patience to make it through the months ahead. Then God's peace came over me and my problems began to seem as if they were very small. I learned that if I put my faith in God, his peace and comfort would allow me to enjoy life during my time of need. This breakthrough allowed me to experience a greater level of faith in God. It also showed me how small our problems are, and how easily they are dealt with when we let God handle them.

Lord, grant us the wisdom and common sense that we need so we will not work our way into so much debt that we have a terrible time trying to get out of it. If a financial problem happens to fall in our laps, please grant us the patience and peace we need to carry on and enjoy life. Help us always to remember that you are a Father to us and that you are protecting and providing for us and help us to always listen to and follow your direction for our lives.

Philippians 4:19

But my God shall supply all your need according to his riches in glory by Christ Jesus.

1 Timothy 6:10–12

For the love of money is the root of all evil: which while some coveted after, they have erred from the faith, and pierced themselves through with many sorrows. But thou, O man of God, flee these things; and follow after righteousness, godliness, faith, love, patience, meekness. Fight the good fight of faith, lay hold on eternal life, whereunto thou art also called, and hast professed a good profession before many witnesses.

Psalms 29:11

The Lord will give strength unto his people; the Lord will bless his people with peace.

Deuteronomy 11:13–17

And it shall come to pass, if ye shall hearken diligently unto my commandments which I command you this day, to love the Lord your God, and to serve him with all your heart and with all your soul, that I will give you the rain of your land in his due season, the first rain and the latter rain, that thou mayest gather in thy corn, and thy wine, and thine oil. And I will send grass in thy fields for thy cattle, that thou mayest eat and be full. Take heed to yourselves, that your heart be not deceived, and ye turn aside, and serve other gods, and worship them; and then the Lord's wrath be kindled against you, and he shut up the heaven, that there be no rain, and that the land yield not her fruit; and lest ye perish quickly from off the good land which the Lord giveth you.

The Consequences of Prayer

Have you ever prayed and wondered why the answer to your prayer has not yet come to pass? Have your prayers ever been answered in a way that you never expected? Sometimes when we pray we don't realize what we are actually asking God to do. Sometimes it takes many years for a prayer to be answered. At other times your prayer may have been answered, but in a way that you didn't expect. When we pray and ask God to intervene in our situation, many times we have an idea of how God might answer our prayer. More often than not, God has a totally different way of answering our prayers from what we expected. One example of this just happens to come to mind.

One day as I was going through my morning routine, Monday morning routine to be exact, and was feeling a little woozy, I sat down on the couch for a few minutes to rest. I didn't know why I was feeling bad and thought I might feel better if I just rested for a while. After a few minutes, I started feeling a little better, so I decided to eat breakfast. My wife was up by now and saw me hunched over and looking pitiful while I was eating. "Honey, are you all right?" she asked. "Your face looks pale."

I told her I didn't feel very good and that I would be all right if I could get some energy. About halfway through breakfast, I started feeling woozy again, only this time it was worse.

I went back to the couch and just sat there for a few minutes and prayed. I prayed that whatever was causing me to feel that way would just go away. I didn't want to have to try to go to work feeling bad and was afraid it might affect my driving. I didn't have any sick days accumulated yet at my new job and I didn't want to lose a day's wages. I kept telling God that I had to go to work, like he didn't already know that, and to please take this pain away. I felt a little better after praying, so I went back to eating. A little while later, I started feeling woozy again, except this time I had a funny feeling in the pit of my stomach and in my throat. *Oh, no,* I thought, *I'm not going to do what I think I am going to do, am I? I haven't done that in many years.* Sure enough, I went into the bathroom and had a face-to-face meeting with our toilet bowl! EEEEEYYYUCK!!!!!! Fifteen minutes later I felt like a new person and was actually ready for the long drive to work. I knew I could make it now. My prayer had been answered, but in a way that I didn't expect and that I really would not have preferred.

Prayers are not always answered so quickly, and many times our prayers are answered in a way that we may not understand. Sometimes our prayers are actually answered and we don't realize it until many years later when something jogs our memory back to that particular prayer. Then we can see exactly what God has done and the method he used to answer our prayer. As the old saying goes, "Hindsight is twenty-twenty." Even though some situations may seem hopeless at times and some people who may be in your prayers seem as if they will never change, just keep the faith up and remember that God often works in ways that we do not understand. Some day something will happen that will allow you to see that person in a whole new light. That is when something will click on the inside of you and you will see how your prayers were answered. Through prayer you really can make a difference in your life as well as the lives of those around you. So whether you are praying for your spouse to change, or for your friend to be more understanding of you, or for that special problem person who needs to get a whole new outlook on life, or even the salvation of another person, no matter what the circumstances may be, God is greater than our situation and God is working in our situation. We may or may not have quick results, but one day when we least expect it, a miracle will take place and our prayer will be answered! Just remember to hang in there with faith, keep up the hope, and do your best to deposit as much love into your situation as you can (1 Corinthians 13:13).

Philippians 4:6

Be careful for nothing; but in every thing by prayer and supplication with thanksgiving let your requests be made known unto God.

Mark 11:24

Therefore I say unto you, What things soever ye desire, when ye pray, believe that ye receive them, and ye shall have them.

Matthew 21:22

And all things, whatsoever ye shall ask in prayer, believing, ye shall receive.

Matthew 6:5–7

And when thou prayest, thou shalt not be as the hypocrites are: for they love to pray standing in the synagogues and in the corners of the streets, that they may be seen of men. Verily I say unto you, They have their reward. But thou, when thou prayest, enter into thy closet, and when thou hast shut thy door, pray to the Father which is in secret; and thy Father which seeth in secret shall reward thee openly. But when ye pray, use not vain repetitions, as the heathen do: for they think that they shall be heard for their much speaking. Be not ye therefore like unto them: for your Father knoweth what things ye have need of, before ye ask him.

Luke 6:28

Bless them that curse you, and pray for them which despitefully use you.

James 5:16

Confess your faults one to another, and pray one for another, that ye may be healed. The effectual fervent prayer of a righteous man availeth much.

Three

Patience Is a Virtue/Being Put to the Test

Wouldn't it be nice if we could walk into God's personal library, pull out a book about our lives, and read about what will happen next? Life would be much easier on us because we could prepare ourselves for what is about to take place. Take my wife, for example. If I had known that she was the woman I would marry, I would not have worried about dating any other women. It seemed that the women I wanted to date were already dating someone. I was tired of the dating scene and was ready to give it up for a while. That was when we met and something inside me said that she was the right woman for me. She had just broken off a relationship with someone, so we were off to a shaky start. She wasn't ready to jump right into another relationship. It was also hard for us to get together on the same night because she worked evenings and I worked during the day. We managed to go on one or two dates every month. Talk about taking it slow. Somewhere there must have been a couple of turtles getting off to a faster start than we were. I knew she was the right woman for me, so I tried to be patient, yet persistent so she would know that I was still interested in seeing her.

After five months of hit-and-miss dating, I was getting tired of trying. It seemed that the only one doing the calling and the chasing was me. I never knew if she really liked me or not. I decided to forget about her and move on with my life. Two months went by and she realized that I wasn't calling her anymore. Finally, God woke her up in the middle of the night and told her that I was the friend she had been wanting and if she did not give me a chance, then she would lose me. This was about the time I was considering giving her one last chance. I didn't want to call her right away and kept putting it off, thinking maybe someone else would come along soon. Finally, to my surprise, she called me! I couldn't believe it! This was the first time she ever called me. We started dating and this time everything went much better.

Things finally worked out for us even though we were very close to losing each other. As always, God knew what was going on and his timing is what brought us together. One of the biggest keys to letting God work in your life is having the patience it takes to wait on his timing. Does anyone out there have any patience they can loan me? Sometimes I have a lot of patience, but at other times, it seems I don't have enough. Lord, please grant us the patience we need to make it through our future struggles.

Isaiah 40:31

But they that wait upon the Lord shall renew their strength; they shall mount up with wings as eagles: they shall run, and not be weary; and they shall walk, and not faint.

Psalms 40:1

I waited patiently for the Lord; and he inclined unto me, and heard my cry.

Many times in life we are tested by God to prove to him that we really want him to be in control of our lives. Most of the time, it involves having to sacrifice something in life. It may seem like a huge sacrifice to make at the time, but after everything is over, you will realize that God has actually helped you out in life. Sometimes I picture God as someone who is trimming a bush and my life is that bush. Whenever my life starts to get out of control, God comes along, carefully trims away the unwanted things, and helps me stay within my boundaries so I can continue to be what he wants me to be.

At one point in my life, there was a situation in which God did a lot of trimming in my life. It was during this time that God was telling me to "shape up or ship out." He was telling me to stop living for him seventy percent of the time and start living for him one hundred percent of the time or not at all. It was horrible finding out that God would have to ask this of me, but then I realized that I had been fooling myself in my walk with God. I wasn't spending time with him in prayer and had gotten away from reading my Bible. This was causing me to become very selfish.

One of the areas I was having problems in was at work. My drafting supervisor had been turning into a tyrant. He had become the kind of boss who was following the drafters everywhere and looking over our shoulders to make sure we were working. I'm sure you know the type. It was driving me bonkers because I was sick of working for those types of people. I had also been getting burned out in drafting for the past three years. It was getting boring. I could do my job with my eyes closed. I was now becoming very bitter towards my job, and it was affecting my life. It was then that God was trying to remind me that if there is anything in our lives that we cannot deal with and, keeps us from our walk with him, then we should remove that thing from our life. I had been investing in the stock market for the previous four months and had almost tripled my money. It seemed that it would be easy to make a living investing as long as a close watch was kept on everything. I decided to leave my job to give it a try. I felt this was the only way I could live for God one hundred percent, as he wanted me to. I was having such a hard time at work that I could not and did not desire to work out the problems of the situation. Another area that I felt God had been directing me in was to attend a church that my wife and I had left a few years earlier. It seemed that God was telling me that he had something very important planned for me at that particular church. I wasn't quite sure what it was, but I just knew there was something there. It was hard for me to do this because I truly enjoyed the church that we were currently attending. Reluctantly, I told God that if this was what he wanted me to do, I would be more than willing to pursue it. It wasn't very much later when we started attending our old church.

After one month passed, things became very shaky with many ups and downs until we began to lose more money than we were gaining. I thought I had done what God wanted me to do with my drafting job. I had also been spending about three hours a day reading my Bible and praying that God would continue to reveal to me his plan for my life. But, this time my desire was more than just what I felt was the right thing to do. I wanted a real answer from God. I wanted something that was absolutely one hundred percent from God. Since we had purposely not mentioned anything to anyone about what was going on in my life, we were amazed at what happened next. About a week later, a friend of mine, who was one of the elders at the church we had returned to, came to me and told me that he had received a prophecy from the Lord about me. Here is what he said. . . .

Todd,
Whatever circumstances God used to bring you back to this church was for his purpose, to work in your life in a greater measure.

The Lord is preparing a ministry for you. He has called you to do something different, something unusual yet exciting, and something greater than you ever could have imagined. It is probably different than what you imagined, but nonetheless, a ministry that is great in his sight and perfect for you.

Sometimes we feel we have been forgotten by the Lord, as you may feel. But the waiting is a time of perfecting, a time of maturing, a time of learning. So don't fear, Todd, the Lord of Hosts is with you and soon he will reveal himself to you in a new way.

Be obedient, be committed, and trust in the Lord, for soon your ministry will be revealed and he shall accomplish through you that thing he has prepared for you.

I believe this was a true prophecy from God because it confirmed that everything I had done so far was the right thing to do. Also, there was no way my friend could have known what I had been going through. We hadn't even told our family about anything yet. I still thought that my future was in investing our money in the stock market until the big one happened a couple of weeks later. We had a stock go sour on us and we lost money on it. We ended up with the same amount of money we had when we first started to invest in stocks.

I began to consider going back to work at my old job, not that I would turn my back on what I thought God wanted me to do, but to be able to have the steady income that we needed rather than the roller-coaster ride. I believe now that God wanted me to prove to him that I could put my past job experience behind me and show that I was willing to work there in spite of the bad environment. It was a very humbling experience, having to ask for my old job back when I was not very excited about returning to work there. For some reason the paperwork had not yet been done the way it normally is when someone leaves a government job and they told me they might not have an opening for a drafter for about three or four months. We all know how the government works. Turtle speed. This was God's way of telling me to keep hanging in there and that things would work out. I needed to have peace from God now more than ever, so I fasted two meals a day for two weeks and sought God for a more specific answer as to what to do with my life. Naturally, after everything that had just taken place, I wasn't sleeping very well at all.

One day my wife was encouraging me, as she has so many times in the past, to go back to college. This was something I had pondered in the past, but I always thought it wasn't worth it because drafting had always provided me with a good job having a reasonable income. I picked up her college catalog and began looking through it. A business degree had always sounded interesting to me, so I paged through that area of the catalog. After a few minutes of dwelling on the subject, I felt at peace with it and it seemed that going back to college could possibly be what God wanted me to do. The next couple of nights I slept like a baby and each day I became more excited about the possibility of returning to college.

As I look back over what took place, everything that has happened up to this point seemed to make so much sense. This was the second time in my life that I had no intention of attending college. In order for me to think about attending college, it was necessary for me to leave my drafting job and not be able to return. Also, our stocks had to lose money so I would begin to lose the desire of investing for a living. If everything would have worked with the stocks, I would not have had any desire to attend college. It was also essential for me to know that God might want me to return to college. Since my desire is to do God's will in my life, that replaced my old desire to avoid going back to college. I became more excited than ever about attending college because I truly believed the answer to my unhappiness could be found in trying another avenue in life. It seemed at this point in my life that the only way it would be worthwhile for me to return to college would be if I could somehow find some financial assistance.

My wife worked for a major corporation, and she informed me that if I could get on there at an entry-level position, the company would provide excellent benefits toward helping pay for a college education. Since my wife worked at the company, I knew how great it would be to be one of their employees and I felt it would be a great opportunity for me if I could just get my foot in the door. I thought it surely couldn't hurt to try. Sometimes all you can do when you believe God may be leading you in a particular direction in life is to attempt to go in that direction and see what happens. If that is truly where God is taking you, all of the right doors will open for you to go in that direction. Knowing this I proceeded onward with my newfound possibility.

I applied for an entry-level position in their printing department. I was one of about forty applicants for the job. I made it through the initial interview and found that they were going to choose between me and four other people to fill the position. I thought I had done very well in my second interview, but the one catch that got me was this. I would have to accept a wage making two dollars per hour less than I could make in the field of drafting. I didn't mind this at all because the portion of college expenses that the company would meet would more than make up for my loss in pay. I explained this to the people who interviewed me, because their worst fear was that I would not be satisfied with the pay and that I would return to drafting for a living. I tried to explain to them how I felt I was in a dead-end job and that I had gone just about as far as I could as a drafter and that I truly did not wish to pursue a career in drafting.

After all of my efforts, I still didn't convince them. They still seemed to think I would leave after three or four months for a higher paying job. They couldn't understand how I looked at getting my foot in the door as an investment in my future. As a result, they ended up hiring someone else to fill the position. Boy, was I upset. Once again a dream of mine had been crushed by something I had no control over.

So now what could I do? What choices did I have? There didn't seem to be very many and what few there were seemed to be diminishing very rapidly. I wondered where God was leading me and why I couldn't seem to find the direction he wanted me to go. I ended up finding another drafting job and questioned whether it was the right thing to do.

I didn't realize it at the time, but in everything I had tried prior to finding that drafting job there was an attempt towards taking the easy way out. This is something that we all try to do whenever we go through a troublesome time in our life. We tend to say, "All right, God, I've learned my lesson. It's time to move on now." Do these words sound familiar? Perhaps at one time or another, we have all said the very same thing during our childhood. At least anyone who got into trouble as a child has at one time or another "coined" these very phrases.

For instance, say you snuck off and got into the cookie jar. There's just something about children and cookies. It's kind of like the potato chip company's saying you can't just eat one chip without wanting another. The next thing you know, you have devoured the whole bag of potato chips, or in this case cookies. We all know what happens next. Whether you were caught by your parents with your hand in the cookie jar or not, sooner or later your mistake catches up with you and you get sick from eating all those cookies. As you are experiencing the pain that came as a result of the choice you made to eat all those cookies, you end up saying something like, "All right, I've learned my lesson. Just take this pain away and I will never eat that many cookies again."

Tough situations such as this tend to bring about serious words of regret. However, the effect is not always a lasting one.

31

Time goes on and eventually you forget about that experience you had. You once again feel that urge come upon you to raid the cookie jar. You know that your favorite cookies are just sitting there waiting for you to devour them. Once again you give in and you end up eating all of the cookies that are in the jar. Later on when you least expect it, you get sick a second time because of all those cookies you ate. This time it becomes a more lasting memory because as you begin to experience those same pains all over again, you remember the other time it happened to you.

Normally at this point, you have learned a lesson that you will never forget, although for some it takes a few more trips to the cookie jar. Eventually, we all come to the same conclusion and the mistake we made stays in our long-term memory as one that we never wish to experience again. We keep ourselves disciplined so that we don't allow ourselves to ever make the same mistake again. The driving force behind our discipline is the fact that we remember our past experiences and take them into consideration for our future reference.

This story relates well to what I went through in my career as a drafter. I had worked for many people who had been cut from the same mold. When I would get tired of trying to deal with them, I would just take the easy way out by finding another job. I would always receive a better paying job from the next company, so I had a way of justifying my decision to leave. It seemed to me that I had gone as far as I possibly could as a drafter, and even though I questioned whether I was doing the right thing in taking on another drafting job, God knew all along what he was up to. By now you could probably guess what happened next.

After a few months at my new job, I found once again that I was working for another person with the same type of personality as my previous bosses. However, this person was the king of all impossible people to work for. He knew how to crack a whip and really make it snap. I decided to try to stick it out for a while because the company offered an unlimited amount of overtime. After a while, it finally dawned on me what God was doing with my life. I had not yet totally learned how to deal with these types of people, and God was slowly teaching me. This time was different from the rest because we needed to pay off a bunch of bills, and the unlimited amount of overtime was too good to turn down. The only problem with this was the fact that the more overtime I worked, the more encounters I had with my boss. I was stuck in a position in which it seemed I had no choice.

All right, let's add up what we now know to be true at this point. God closes the doors to places where he doesn't want us to go in life; therefore He must open the door that he wants us to go through. I didn't think my current drafting job was what God wanted me to do with my life. I just looked at it as a way to pay off our bills and get out of debt. God looked at it as a potential teaching experience for him, which on my end becomes a learning experience from the school of hard knocks. This would be the learning experience, which would develop discipline for me, or in other words, my final trip to the cookie jar.

As time went on, the problem on my end began to escalate. Since I was working overtime all week long, my weekends at home were filled with getting caught up on chores around the house. I barely had any time to rest, let alone spend any quality time reading my Bible. I wasn't spending any time in prayer nor was I getting anything out of the church that we were attending. I felt as if I had been stripped of everything in my life and forced out into the wilderness. I was a prime target for the devil to shoot at, and he certainly threw everything he could at me.

I began to develop a bitter attitude towards my boss and some of my coworkers. I was upset with our financial situation. I was upset because my weekends were full of work. I was upset because I felt I was headed in a direction away from God rather than where I knew he wanted me to be in life. I was upset because I was at a dying church and couldn't get anything out of the services. There seemed to be many reasons upon reasons to be upset, and there didn't seem to be a light at the end of the tunnel. Every facet of my life just made me more and more upset and only added fuel to the fire. My flame of temper began to burn hotter and hotter, and my attitude grew more bitter with every tick of the clock. Everything escalated so quickly that I lost total control. The only way out for me was to call out desperately for God to intervene in my situation. I ran to God as fast as I could and he began working on me. He gave me peace and patience and taught me to be forgiving of others even as I was experiencing the pain and grief they brought upon me. With God's help I was able to hold out until I received the blessing that he had in store for me.

Even though I had experienced a breakthrough and God was able to discipline my attitude, I still wanted to leave my current job. But this time it was for a different reason. This time I just wanted whatever God had in store for me. I wanted a job in which I could have the freedom to make my own design decisions and the space necessary to do my job without the stress of someone constantly staring over my shoulder. I wanted to work at a company in which I felt I was a worthwhile employee who had the respect of his peers. I wanted all this, but I would have been happy with just finding a stress-free job. I laid my desires in God's hands and left it at that. From then on I just tried to keep up the positive attitude that with God's help, all things are possible. I also kept my attitude in the workplace as pleasant and disciplined as I possibly could. A few months later, God blessed me with a new job. Not only did he give me a stress-free environment to work in, but he gave me all of the other things I had desired for in a job. I was so happy I thought I had died and gone to Heaven.

This experience in life brought about a greater appreciation for all God has blessed me with in life. It also helped me realize that God is in control of our lives even when we think we are going the wrong direction. After having this experience, I could certainly relate to the Bible story that tells of Jesus Christ when he was out in the wilderness being tempted by the devil. That is exactly what had just happened to me. And just as Jesus was able to come out of his situation victoriously, the grace of God was able to carry me through my situation victoriously. The key was the point at which I let go and gave the problem I had been wrestling with to God. Then, as he helped me apply forgiveness to the situation, I was able to pass the test and receive the blessing of my current job. This was one of those trials in life that made me appreciate the poem "Footprints." The following describes what the poem says:

Footprints

One night a man had a dream. He dreamed he was walking along a beach with the Lord. Across the sky flashed scenes from his life. At first he noticed two sets of footprints in the sand; one belonged to him and the other to the Lord.

When the last scene of his life flashed before him, he looked back at the footprints in the sand. He noticed that many times along the path of his life there was only one set of footprints. He also noticed that this happened at the very lowest and saddest times in his life.

This really bothered him and he questioned the Lord about it. "Lord, you said that once I decided to follow you, you'd walk with me all the way. But I have noticed that during the most troublesome times in my life, there is only one set of footprints. I don't understand why, when I needed you most, you would leave me."

The Lord replied, "My precious, precious child, I love you and would never leave you. During your times of trial and suffering, when you see only one set of footprints, it was then that I carried you."

I had just gone through one of those situations in my life that the poem talks about. It was one of those situations in which God picked me up and carried me through my struggle, even though I couldn't seem to find the strength to go on. As a result, the first thing I did when I went to my new job was to stick a nail in the wall and hang a large picture from it, which also had the words from the "Footprints" poem. This would serve as a constant reminder to me of how faithful God was to me when I needed him. This also is a reminder to me to stay committed to God and to apply his forgiveness to every situation in my life.

Learning to apply God's forgiveness to our lives is a vital part of life as a Christian. There are numerous stories in the Bible in which you find Jesus teaching by example how to apply forgiveness to all situations. If we were to never learn forgiveness, then we could not advance with God's plan for our lives. However, if we do learn forgiveness, then we are opening a whole new door for God to pour out blessings upon our lives. It is our responsibility as Christians to apply God's forgiveness and grace to the various circumstances throughout our lives. As for everything else that is out of our control, we just have to let the chips fall where they may. One thing I have learned through this trial is that every time God tests you in life, you always come out of it a much stronger person for having greater faith in God.

James 1:2–4

My brethren, count it all joy when ye fall into divers temptations; Knowing this, that the trying of your faith worketh patience. But let patience have her perfect work, that ye may be perfect and entire, wanting nothing.

Mark 11:25–26

And when ye stand praying, forgive, if ye have ought against any: that your Father also which is in heaven may forgive you your trespasses. But if ye do not forgive, neither will your Father which is in heaven forgive your trespasses.

Luke 6:37

Judge not, and ye shall not be judged: condemn not, and ye shall not be condemned: forgive, and ye shall be forgiven:

Luke 17:3, 4

Take heed to yourselves: If thy brother trespass against thee, rebuke him; and if he repent, forgive him. And if he trespass against thee seven times in a day, and seven times in a day turn again to thee, saying, I repent; thou shalt forgive him.

Job 23:10–12

But he knoweth the way that I take: when he hath tried me, I shall come forth as gold. My foot hath held his steps, his way have I kept, and not declined. Neither have I gone back from the commandment of his lips; I have esteemed the words of his mouth more than my necessary food.

Four
Shame on You

One of the problems in the world today is the fact that too many Christians choose to shelter themselves from the outside world. Many of them also do not want to do what is necessary to be committed in their walk with God throughout their life. When it comes to conduct, they act like a bunch of babies who can't even get along with other Christians, and they grow to rely upon a spoon-fed gospel from their pastor. Anytime they need help, they cry out to their pastors, "Feed me, feed me." Their pastor feeds them with the gospel and they go home feeling good about themselves, which was what they wanted. When babies act like babies and they get what they want, all this does is reinforce their behavior.

Many people in the world today act like babies. They cry and whine until they are given what they want. As the old saying goes, the squeaky wheel always gets the grease. That is to say, the person who cries the loudest gets what he wants before anyone else does, just so others don't have to listen to the baby crying anymore. Since many Christians act this way because they are spiritually immature, this gives them a bad witness to the rest of the world. The world sees them as people who claim to be Christians, but are truly hypocrites in their actions and their lifestyles. When the rest of the world sees this, they see no benefit to Christianity. Who wants to go to a church where many people can't even get along with each other and all they do is act like a bunch of babies? Then, when it really comes down to it, they don't even live what they say they believe in. How could this sort of life be attractive to anyone?

We serve such a graceful God that he puts up with many people who act like babies. God is such a great God that he allows us to make many choices to live our lives the way we want to. You can choose to shelter yourself from the outside world, or you can choose to stand right in the middle of the outside world and shine the light of Jesus to a lost and dying world in need of direction. Which do you think God would want you to do?

If we were to look at the example that Jesus Christ set in the Bible, we would come to realize that God would want us to shine the light of Jesus to all of the world. It is our calling in life. Yet, many people choose to go home feeling good about themselves because they have been spiritually fed in a church service and they don't bother to share anything they have learned in life with other people. If they do share what they know with other people, it is usually people they know who are also Christians. In other words, they only talk to the kind of people whom they feel comfortable around. What kind of a witness is that? That isn't a witness. That is keeping what you know confined to your own little circle of friends. That is only opening up yourself to people who will not make fun of you for who you are. As a result, your own insecurities keep you from ever doing what God wants all Christians to do, which is to be a witness to others. How can we ever be a witness to others if we keep our Christian lives hidden from the rest of the world?

If you are the kind of person whom I am speaking about, I would like to challenge you to rise up to be a good Christian witness to the rest of the world. Grow up and live your life the way you say you believe, and don't be afraid to let others find out about it. If you are afraid of being an outcast, just remember that God will never leave us or forsake us. Learn to rely on the strength of God rather than your own strength. Those who are going to cast you out for living your life the way you believe really aren't being true friends to you anyway. If they aren't a true friend to you, their friendship doesn't hold any value at all. Cast your cares upon God, and he will give you comfort in your time of need.

If you truly desire to be a positive Christian witness to others, there may be a few things you need to realize first. There are many mistakes people make in their attempts to witness to others. One example I mentioned earlier was being pushy and bothering people all the time. Don't be pushy. All it does is turn people off and they end up running from you. Jesus Christ said he wanted to make us "fishers of men." How many fishermen have you seen who catch any fish by chasing them around and bothering them all of the time? On the other hand, how many fishermen have you seen who cast out bait for the fish, and patiently reel the bait in as they attempt to lure the fish to the bait. That is how God wants us to be effective witnesses for him. When the opportunity presents itself, we can toss out a phrase into the air about the Bible or Christianity. Then we can see if we get a nibble. If we don't, we can always try again at a later date. If we do interest someone in what we have said, all that does is open the door for us to be able to talk with him or her about Christianity. Since we now have aroused their curiosity, they will listen more intently to what we have to say.

One other common mistake people make, which keeps them from being able to witness to others, is that they do not like being around any sinners because they don't care for the way a sinner acts. We can't expect someone to act a certain way before we will even attempt to witness to them. Sinners are sinners and they shouldn't be expected to behave any differently than they already behave. If you don't like the way a sinner acts, grow up and deal with it. You can't effectively witness to a person when you are making it obvious that you don't really want to be around them. Nobody should expect a sinner to act like anything but a sinner, because that is exactly what sinners are. Don't condemn them for living their lives the way they choose. At least they aren't a bunch of hypocrites. They live their lives according to what they believe in. Boy, could some Christians in this world take an example from them. Just imagine if all the people in this world who claimed to be Christians had a lifestyle that truly reflected their beliefs. Just imagine the impact it would have on a world that is seeking for answers. Christians would be forgiving rather than judgmental. Christians would accept sinners for who they are, and not condemn or harass them. Christians would be showing the true love of Jesus Christ to the world.

I believe this would have a profound effect on many people. I believe that this would only attract people to Christianity. They would naturally be attracted to the light of a great, loving, and caring God that is alive inside us. We need to follow the example of Jesus Christ and go out into the world and shine the light of truth. That is the only way we will ever have an impact on the world we live in. A prime example of this is the example of two different churches that have tried in their own way to reach out to the communities around them. I will not mention their names. I will only refer to them as Church Number One and Church Number Two.

The pastor of Church Number One has a desire for his church to be a light in its community. He wants it to be a church that will attract sinners to Jesus Christ. The people of Church Number One say they have the same desire, but many of their intentions seem to prove otherwise. Many of them are faithful church attendees. I'm sure there are some people who are sincere in their desire to reach out to the community around them, but they honestly don't know how to go about accomplishing their goal. Instead, they go on with their lives and choose to do nothing about the mission. This church has the same people attending it every week. There are a few new faces from time to time, and there are many services in which you can truly sense the presence of God.

Once all is said and done, though, and it comes down to the rubber meeting the road, the people of this church barely do anything even to let the community around them know that there is a church in the area. One time they honestly tried to reach out to their community. They attempted to witness to their community by distributing videotapes about the life of Jesus Christ to all who would accept them. Many of the people in this church did not understand why most of the people in the community didn't want their free videotapes. I'm sure there are many reasons why people didn't want the gift, but perhaps the biggest reason is that the people in the community had never heard of that church before. They never had any contact with people from this church before, so they didn't know anything about the true intentions of this church. They probably thought that this church was just another one of those churches that go around trying to force their views upon other people. Since they weren't certain that this church was truly acting in their interest, they weren't receptive to the gift that this church had to offer them.

The pastor of Church Number Two also has a desire for his church to be a light in its community. He also wants it to be a church that will attract sinners to Jesus Christ. The people of Church Number Two, unlike the people of Church Number One, truly do have an honest desire to reach out to their community. They do things for their community, like helping single mothers get their oil changed for free. Throughout the year they go to various parks around the city that they live in and cook hamburgers and hot dogs. Then, they show the light of Jesus Christ by giving the food away free to other people who happen to be in the park that day. They get to know the people and proceed to witness to them. Every Christmas, the people of this church put their money towards hundreds of turkeys, potatoes, vegetables, and other foods.

Then, they rent a large banquet hall and invite the people in their community who could not otherwise afford a decent Christmas meal to come to the banquet hall for a free Christmas dinner. The people of Church Number Two do all of the cooking, cleaning, and waiting on tables. Talk about a witness to your community! People respond to this act of kindness much better because they realize that this church is honestly making an effort to reach out to them. I guarantee that if the people of Church Number Two offered videotapes about the life of Jesus Christ to the people of their community whom they have been witnessing to, many of the people would be receptive to the gift. Why? Because the people of the community have had prior experiences with the people of Church Number Two and they know that the people of Church Number Two have a genuine interest in them.

The sooner that more churches start acting like Church Number Two, the sooner we as Christians will have a greater impact on the world around us. We can't expect the world to change if we aren't willing to do anything about it. If more churches were making an honest effort to witness to their surrounding communities much as Church Number Two has, we would be able to see many lives transformed by Jesus Christ. However, if we choose to act like Church Number One, and we attempt to reach out to our communities without demonstrating a genuine interest in them, we will have the door shut in our faces much the way traveling salesmen have. We would offer them something up front for free, but they would wonder if our general interest was truly in their well-being, or whether this was just another feeble attempt at a good deed by someone who is going through the motions of some religious doctrine. They would not accept our gift because they have never been shown that we genuinely care about them.

We can only make a difference when we personally make an effort to show them that we do genuinely care about them. It can only be made when we choose to reach out and touch the lives of others. Occupying a seat in a church building isn't going to cut it. Putting money in the offering plate isn't going to cut it. Waiting for someone else to do it isn't going to cut it. Being judgmental and condemning sinners for being sinners isn't going to cut it. Telling someone his hair is too long isn't going to cut it. If God didn't like long hair, he wouldn't have placed the key to Samson's strength in his hair and told Samson never to cut his hair. Telling someone he or she has to be dressed a certain way before he can even consider going to church isn't going to cut it. Telling someone he or she has the wrong color of skin isn't going to cut it.

The Bible says in Titus 2:11 and also in Hebrews 5:9 that salvation is for all who would receive it. "All" is a very broad category, if you ask me, and it is very obvious that it includes all human beings, no matter who they are, where they are from, what color their skin is, or what kind of lives they have lived. If you really want to reach out to people, don't look at them as they appear in the natural. Look at them through the eyes of Jesus Christ and see them as they can be. Then, look at yourself as the possibility of being the bridge that closes the gap between them and Jesus Christ. All you have to do is be a good witness in your life and show them that you truly care. They will see the light of Jesus Christ shining in your life, and when they are ready, they will either cross the bridge on their own or ask you to help them cross the bridge. Why? Because people are naturally attracted to the light of Jesus Christ.

We cannot expect people to see the light of Jesus Christ just by our mere presence in the same room with them. We must do something to reach out to them. Help them move, mow their lawn, shovel their driveway, or buy them lunch. Many times you will find that all people want is someone who will listen to them without condemning them. Go ahead, take that first step and let the light of Jesus Christ shine through you in your actions. Your actions witness to people more than you may think, because these are what reveal the true intentions of your heart. You will never regret the choice you make to witness to others in this manner. You truly can make a difference if you just try a little.

If it is our honest intention to make a difference in the world around us, it will all start with a choice that we must make. We must choose to be the kind of witness that can make a difference. We must make the choice to reach out to others and bridge the gap that lies between you. This is exactly what Jesus Christ did when he chose to come into this world. Jesus extended himself, and chose to be our ultimate sacrifice so that we might all have a way to be cleansed from our sin. Jesus chose to bridge the gap between us and God so that we could find a way back to God. Jesus was not forced by God to go through anything he didn't want to do. Jesus chose to do what he did, and now we as Christians have the same choice to be able to do just as Jesus did.

I like to look at it this way. Jesus came into this world and went through all of the suffering, pain, and endurance of temptation, yet he still remained without sin. Then, he finished it off by dying a sacrificial death so that we could be set free from the bondage of sin. The least that I can do for Jesus Christ, since he went through all of that just for me, is to dedicate my life to be used by him for whatever purpose he wishes.

1 Corinthians 9:14

Even so hath the Lord ordained that they which preach the gospel should live of the gospel.

Proverbs 11:9

A hypocrite with his mouth destroyeth his neighbour: but through knowledge shall the just be delivered.

Luke 6:20–49

And he lifted up his eyes on his disciples, and said, Blessed be ye poor: for yours is the kingdom of God. Blessed are ye that hunger now: for ye shall be filled. Blessed are ye that weep now: for ye shall laugh. Blessed are ye, when men shall hate you, and when they shall separate you from their company, and shall reproach you, and cast out your name as evil, for the Son of man's sake. Rejoice ye in that day, and leap for joy: for, behold, your reward is great in heaven: for in the like manner did their fathers unto the prophets.

But woe unto you that are rich! for ye have received your consolation. Woe unto you that are full! for ye shall hunger. Woe unto you that laugh now! for ye shall mourn and weep. Woe unto you, when all men shall speak well of you! for so did their fathers to the false prophets. But I say unto you which hear, Love your enemies, do good to them which hate you, Bless them that curse you, and pray for them which despitefully use you. And unto him that smiteth thee on the one cheek offer also the other; and him that taketh away thy cloke forbid not to take thy coat also. Give to every man that asketh of thee; and of him that taketh away thy goods ask them not again.

And as ye would that men should do to you, do ye also to them likewise. For if ye love them which love you, what thank have ye? for sinners also love those that love them. And if ye do good to them which do good to you, what thank have ye? for sinners also do even the same. And if ye lend to them of whom ye hope to receive, what thank have ye? for sinners also lend to sinners, to receive as much again. But love ye your enemies, and do good, and lend, hoping for nothing again; and your reward shall be great, and ye shall be the children of the Highest: for he is kind unto the unthankful and to the evil. Be ye therefore merciful, as your Father also is merciful. Judge not, and ye shall not be judged: condemn not, and ye shall not be condemned: forgive, and ye shall be forgiven: Give, and it shall be given unto you; good measure, pressed down, and shaken together, and running over, shall men give into your bosom. For with the same measure that ye mete withal it shall be measured to you again. And he spake a parable unto them, Can the blind lead the blind? shall they not both fall into the ditch? The disciple is not above his master: but every one that is perfect shall be as his master.

And why beholdest thou the mote that is in thy brother's eye, but perceivest not the beam that is in thine own eye? Either how canst thou say to thy brother, Brother, let me pull out the mote that is in thine eye, when thou thyself beholdest not the beam that is in thine own eye? Thou hypocrite, cast out first the beam out of thine own eye, and then shall thou see clearly to pull out the mote that is in thy brother's eye.

For a good tree bringeth not forth corrupt fruit; neither doth a corrupt tree bring forth good fruit. For every tree is known by his own fruit. For of thorns men do not gather figs, nor of a bramble bush gather they grapes. A good man out of the good treasure of his heart bringeth forth that which is good; and an evil man out of the evil treasure of his heart bringeth forth that which is evil: for of the abundance of the heart his mouth speaketh.

And why call ye me, Lord, Lord, and do not the things which I say? Whosoever cometh to me, and heareth my sayings, and doeth them, I will shew you to whom he is like: He is like a man which built a house, and digged deep, and laid the foundation on a rock: and when the flood arose, the stream beat vehemently upon that house, and could not shake it: for it was founded upon a rock. But he that heareth, and doeth not, is like a man that without a foundation built a house upon the earth; against which the stream did beat vehemently, and immediately it fell; and the ruin of that house was great.

For what is the hope of the hypocrite, though he hath gained, when God taketh away his soul?

James 2:17–26

Even so faith, if it hath not works, is dead, being alone. Yea, a man may say, Thou hast faith, and I have works: shew me thy faith without thy works, and I will shew thee my faith by my works. Thou believest that there is one God; thou doest well: the devils also believe, and tremble. But wilt thou know, O vain man, that faith without works is dead? Was not Abraham our father justified by works, when he had offered Isaac his son upon the altar? Seest thou how faith wrought with his works, and by works was faith made perfect? And the scripture was fulfilled which saith, Abraham believed God, and it was imputed unto him for righteousness: and he was called the Friend of God. Ye see then how that by works a man is justified, and not by faith only. For as the body without the spirit is dead, so faith without works is dead also.

Five

What Christianity and Religion *Really* Are

Have you ever known someone to take something you have said and blow it totally out of proportion? I'm certain that at one time or another, we have all had this happen to us. People hear you say something and they either misunderstand you or they take what you said the wrong way because of their own insecurities or past experiences. Then, they add their perception to your statement and go off telling other people things that are just not true. Without giving you the benefit of the doubt or asking you further questions to realize the true intentions behind your statement, they assume that their perception of your statement is the true way that you intended it to be perceived. When they go talk to other people and add their perception to your statement, other people end up getting a warped perception of what kind of person you really are.

Some people do the exact same thing with the word of God. They add their perception to what the Bible is saying and they end up blowing God's word totally out of proportion. Before long they end up saying something that misrepresents what God was truly saying. Then they go around telling other people things about the Bible that just aren't true. As a result, some of the people they talk to get a warped perception of Christianity, the Bible, or even who God is. Some of those people may never accept Jesus Christ as their Savior. From their point of view, they may think that if they accept Jesus Christ, then they are also accepting the other person's warped beliefs to be true. What many people don't realize is that when they accept Jesus Christ as their Savior, they are not really accepting another person's beliefs. They are simply accepting the fact that God is real and God's word is the truth and that Jesus Christ sacrificed his life for our sins so that we would have a way to repent to God and be cleansed from our sin.

Many people and sects have either distorted the message of salvation through Jesus Christ by adding their own doctrine to what the Bible truly states, or disregarded it as just a bunch of baloney. Then, they go about finding ways to justify their actions. As a result, we now have many "religions" that teach people that they can only gain salvation through doing good works. People belong to a certain branch of religion for many various reasons. Many of them believe that there is obviously only one branch of religion that can be the right one. Therefore, all sects other than the one they observe must be the wrong religion. After all, the form of religion they are currently observing surely must be the right one. Otherwise they wouldn't observe it, right?

Proverbs 12:15 states, "The way of a fool is right in his own eyes: but he that hearkenth unto counsel is wise." What is wrong with this picture? For one thing, if everyone is always right and they all observe a different form of religion, then how can you say that anyone is wrong? On the other hand, if everyone is wrong, how do we know who is really right? Or how could anyone be right? The truth is that there is only one gospel, and all religious sects were started only because people had a difference of opinion, and they couldn't work out their own differences, so they just started their own sects, which incorporated their own beliefs into their doctrine. Remember what I said earlier about blowing something someone said out of proportion? That is what many modern-day forms of "religion" have done.

So how do we know what is truly the right "religion?" If the modern-day definition of religion is defined as a religious attempt to gain salvation by doing good works which is contrary to what the Bible states, then we must refer to the Bible to find the true definition of religion. There just so happens to be a relevant passage in James 1:19–27. Here is what it states:

James 1:19–27

Wherefore, my beloved brethren, let every man be swift to hear, slow to speak, slow to wrath: For the wrath of man worketh not the righteousness of God. Wherefore lay apart all filthiness and superfluity of naughtiness, and receive with meekness the engrafted word, which is able to save your souls. But be ye doers of the word, and not hearers only, deceiving your own selves. For if any be a hearer of the word, and not a doer, he is like unto a man beholding his natural face in a glass: For he beholdeth himself, and goeth his way, and straightway forgetteth what manner of man he was. But whoso looketh into the perfect law of liberty, and continueth therein, he being not a forgetful hearer, but a doer of the work, this man shall be blessed in his deed. If any man among you seem to be religious, and bridleth not his tongue, but deceiveth his own heart, this man's religion is vain. Pure religion and undefiled before God and the Father is this, To visit the fatherless and widows in their affliction, and to keep himself unspotted from the world.

In other words, if you claim to be a religious person, and the words you speak or the actions portraying your lifestyle do not represent the type of person that you say you are, then you are only fooling yourself, and your religion is empty and worthless, and has no real value or significance. Pure religion as defined in this passage is being a doer of the word and remaining unspotted from the world. To put it another way, pure religion is simply living a life without sin and properly conducting in the manner that the Bible states is correct behavior.

Many people just cannot see how anyone could keep one's self "unspotted from the world," as the passage in James states. They truly do not believe that it is possible. Keeping yourself unspotted from the world truly is a tall order and it is one that we certainly cannot accomplish on our own. That is why God sent Jesus Christ into this world. Through the sacrifice Jesus Christ made when he died on the cross, God is now able to meet us right where we are in life. However, this is only possible if we choose to accept the fact that Jesus Christ died to save our souls from sin. That is one thing that makes God so great. He made a way for us to come to him, but as a true father should do, he gives us the choice whether or not we wish to serve him. Once we accept Jesus Christ as our Savior from sin, God begins working on us through other people and situations to draw us closer to becoming someone who is unspotted from the world.

This is another thing that some people and "religions" have backwards. They think that they have to straighten out their lives before God will allow them to be forgiven. We are only human and are born into this world in sin; therefore we do not have the capabilities of cleansing ourselves from sin. That is why Jesus Christ had to come into this world to live a life of perfection and sacrifice his perfect life.

In order to fully understand God's plan for salvation, we must go back in time to where it all began. All of the sins of the world were cast upon man when Adam and Eve disobeyed God in the Garden of Eden. From that point on, man was required to make earthly sacrifices to God in order for their sins to be forgiven. Not only did they have to make a sacrifice, but they had to sacrifice the best that they had in order to prove to

God that they were serious about asking his forgiveness. This usually meant that man had to choose the best sheep of his flock (or whatever the best sacrifice he could make was) and sacrifice that animal's life of innocence in order to be redeemed for his sin. The problem with this was that man had to do this annually, and even though it was the best that could be done, it still wasn't the perfect plan for salvation.

Then, one day that all changed. God sent his only son Jesus into this world, to live a life of perfection. Jesus carried out this task and then gave his life as the eternal sacrifice for man. Jesus was able to be that perfect sacrifice that man needed in order to achieve God's forgiveness. Now through accepting Jesus Christ as our Savior, we are able to trade our sinful, fallen nature for a life filled with happiness, peace, joy, contentment, and best of all eternal salvation and the Kingdom of Heaven. The only way this can be done is to accept the fact that Jesus Christ is truly God's Son, acknowledging that he really did give his life as a sacrifice for us. All we have to do is have the faith it takes to believe this and ask Jesus to come into our hearts and forgive us of our sins and it will be done. When we do that in all sincerity and ask God to forgive us of our sins, God is able to forgive us and we can feel a change take place inside our souls. Something happens and you feel like a brand new person.

Actually, that is really what happens. It's kind of like trading in your old junk heap beater of a car for a sparkling shiny brand new one. But, this is a little different. You are actually trading in your old lifestyle and sinful nature for a new lifestyle and a perfect nature. The only thing you have to do after that is to take care of yourself and live life as God directs you, kind of like taking care of that new car so that it can stay new. The only difference is that eventually, a car will deteriorate anyway, but your salvation through Jesus Christ will never be lost as long as you stay devoted to God. From there on it is up to us to stay committed to God and allow Him to mold us over time into that unspotted person he wants us to be.

My intentions in writing this book are not to try to condemn you or make you feel uncomfortable. It is only my intention to try to let you in on something I found to be true and real. Something to believe in. Something to give you peace when everything else around you is falling apart. It's like having a close buddy who is always with you. Someone you can confide in, laugh with, and just plain enjoy life with. It's sometimes hard to explain how real Jesus is to other people. It's like learning to drive a car. Until you have had the experience, you don't know what it's like. Or how about your favorite dessert? It wasn't your favorite dessert until you tasted it one day. Then you probably wondered why you ever wanted anything else. Give it a try. It certainly won't hurt you. Have faith on Jesus and pray to him. Tell him you believe that he was the Son of God and that he really did sacrifice his life on the cross for our salvation. Ask for forgiveness for your sins and ask Jesus to be Lord in your life. You will find true happiness and your life will be forever changed if you do.

Religion can be a very touchy subject for many people because of what I have tried to explain in this chapter. Many people have this "I am right and you are wrong" mentality and do not want to listen to anyone else. This is what is wrong with a lot of "religions." In fact, many such sects stem from Christianity, but they have broken off and gone their own way, incorporating a doctrine that was thought up by man. Any time you take the word and direction that God has given you and start monkeying around with it, adding things you believe in, and taking out things you don't believe in, you are distorting God's word and direction for your life. By doing this, all people are doing is making their own substitute for God's word. They are taking God's true word and direction, and forcing it to compromise to their own personal beliefs and desires.

There is only one true word and direction from God, and it is up to us to operate in the manner that God wants us to operate. We shouldn't be taking God's word and compromising it to our lifestyle or personal beliefs so that we can feel good about the way we live. This is called justification, and it is wrong. We shouldn't take it upon ourselves to add to or take from the Bible. The Bible was given to us with an Old Testament and a New Testament. Many sects have chosen to throw out the New Testament and say that it doesn't apply. The New Testament teaches the way of salvation through Jesus Christ and many choose not to accept the New Testament because they do not believe that Jesus was the Son of God. Some religions teach that Jesus was just a prophet and that he couldn't have been able to live a perfect life in this world since he was only human. The truth is that Jesus Christ came to earth and took on the form of man. Because he had a direct line of communication abiding with God, he was constantly able to communicate with God and receive the true direction he needed to keep himself from sinning. Jesus Christ was able to live a perfect life without sin. This is the only way our perfect sacrifice could have been made.

Remember the trade I told you about? Adam and Eve traded away their salvation for a life filled with sin when they disobeyed God. How could they get it back? They would have to make a trade back for it, but they couldn't because all that they had was now corrupted by their sin. By Jesus Christ's coming to be the sacrifice we needed, he made the trade for us. He took on all of the sins of man and traded them for his life of perfection. At last, we have a way back to salvation that cannot be changed. By accepting the fact that Jesus Christ died for us, and having the faith it takes to believe this to be true, we can now, through accepting Jesus Christ as our Savior, trade back through Christ our fallen, sinful nature for a new life of salvation. This is where the term "born again" is taken from because the transaction that takes place is one that makes you feel alive, refreshed, and renewed as if you were reborn into this world as a new person. You aren't actually reborn. You just feel the change inside of you, because you feel all of the bad things from your sinful nature being removed from your spirit and all that is left is this wonderful peaceful feeling of salvation.

Sometimes I floor people when they ask me what form of religion I belong to and I tell them that I personally don't observe a form of religion, at least not the modern-day definition of "religion" that I spoke of earlier. I observe pure religion as spoken of in James, chapter one, and everything that the Bible states to be true, which in essence is the true meaning of Christianity. Many people will tell you that Christianity is just another "religion." I have even met Christians who believe that Christianity is a religion because they have bought into the modern-day definition of "religion." This is because they have never really found out that Christianity in its truest form is not a "religion." Nobody ever enlightened them to the fact that it is not a "religion."

Christianity is salvation through Jesus Christ, by which we are made into a new person. We are now given a new life with salvation, or a clean spirit, free of sin. We have traded in our fallen sinful nature and our destiny to rot in the fiery pit of Hell for eternity for a life of happiness, peace, and joy because we have found this in our new life of salvation. Our eternal destiny now becomes that of living with God in the Kingdom of Heaven. If that doesn't excite you, nothing will. Of course, you will not know that excitement unless you know Jesus Christ. And you will not know Jesus Christ unless you accept him as your Savior. Then Jesus will come into the heart of your being, cleanse your soul, and you will have a friend for eternity. That's right, a friend for eternity. Someone whom you can communicate with, and tell all your deepest innermost thoughts and desires to and who will respond to you in a loving, caring way and give you direction for your life. No more pondering life and what it is all about. You will have the answer living right in the very heart of your soul. All you have to do is follow God's direction through Jesus and be obedient to that direction and God's word to us in the Bible, and you will never lose that salvation again.

This is why I say that Christianity is not a "religion," because no actual "religion" tells you that you can have Jesus Christ, the Son of God, living inside your soul, giving you direction for your life. The true definition of modern-day "religion" has no salvation to offer because it basically offers operating to a set of standards and beliefs as a substitute way of salvation. It doesn't include the part where Jesus can redeem us, live inside the heart of our being, and communicate with us. Modern-day "religions" can say anything they want to say, but when it comes right down to it, there is no substitute for the only way of salvation. There is only one way to salvation, and that is through accepting Jesus Christ as our Savior from sin and letting him live inside of us, communicating with us and working on us to make us more like him. What I am trying to show you is that Christianity in its truest form, is not a "religion." It is an ongoing relationship with God, our Heavenly Father, through Jesus Christ, our Savior from sin. Through the communication in this relationship, we can receive guidance and direction for our life, and a happiness that is beyond belief.

I once heard a conversation between two people. One of them was a young man in his twenties. He was explaining to another man who was in his forties his thoughts on religion. This conversation got started because the older gentleman was talking about how he was going to attend the upcoming Easter service at his church. After a few moments of chit-chat, the young man began to open up. He started talking about just recently his wife had started attending a Christian church. She was trying to talk him into going to church with her, but he continued to take a stand that he did not need religion. He told of how he never went to church during his childhood. He went on to say how he had made it this far in life very well without religion. Why would he need religion now? He said that everyone once in a while he felt as if there may be something that he is missing out on in life, but whatever it may be, it certainly wasn't religion.

It may surprise some of you to know that I totally agree with what that young man said. Who needs religion anyway? Of course, I am speaking of the modern-day definition of religion that I mentioned earlier. What does religion really do for people? It might help some people gain more knowledge, but what most modern-day forms of religion have to offer people is just going through a routine that makes them feel better about themselves. Most "religions" only provide an opportunity for people who are simply seeking for a way to justify their actions. They may have done something they shouldn't have done during the past week, but come Saturday or Sunday, everything is all right because they went to church.

Don't take me the wrong way. There are many good things about religion, and going to church. What I'm talking about is going through a weekly routine at church as if it is just another daily routine and somehow this all of the sudden makes you right with God. Some people are totally oblivious to what I am saying, yet they go through the motions of church and "religion" throughout the course of their life thinking they will make it to Heaven when their lives are over. I would like for anyone to show me in the Bible where it says that the only way to get to Heaven is through this "religion," that "religion," or the other "religion." It is sad to see that some people think that other people are right or wrong in their way of thinking because of what religion they belong to. Many people truly believe that other people will never make it to Heaven unless they attend the "right" church, which also happens to be the same church that they are attending. If that church or religion is the only way a person can get to Heaven, what happens when people leave to attend another church or one of a different religious sect? Does this mean they have predestined their souls to eternal damnation? Of course not. This way of thinking is just plain nonsense. Religion never automatically let anyone into Heaven, nor did it send anyone to Hell. In fact, "religion" has been responsible for tearing many people apart because they become stubborn in their differences and they could not be around each other without arguing or holding a grudge. What good does that do? I thought religion was supposed to make us better people? Is that truly a step in the right direction?

The truth is that religion is never solely responsible for making someone a better person. There is only one way a person can make him- or herself a better person just as there is only one way a person can make it to Heaven. Both involve having the personal desire it takes to be a better person and to make the right choices necessary to attain that goal.

God did something amazing in his plan for man. He gave us the choice of how we want to live. He gave us the choice to be who we want to be. Religion cannot save us from Hell, nor can it usher us into Heaven. The only thing that can do this is a choice that we must make. That choice is to accept Jesus Christ as our Savior. The Bible states this fact very clearly. It does not say that the only way to Heaven is through such and such "religion." It says that the only way to Heaven is through accepting Jesus Christ as the Son of God, whom God sent to earth to take on the sins of man and sacrifice his life unto death so that we may obtain life through accepting Jesus Christ as our Savior from sin. When we accept Jesus Christ as our Savior, we enter into a relationship with God through Jesus Christ. It is through this relationship that God is able to speak to our hearts and lead us onward toward truly becoming a better person.

So where does religion fall in all of this? Religion helps reveal to us areas of our lives that we need to work on. Religion offers a means for us to attempt to stay devoted to God. But, religion does not make any choices for us. We must make our own choices. We must choose to accept Jesus Christ as our Savior, and allow a relationship with God through Jesus Christ to lead us onward toward making more correct decisions, which in turn make us a better person. What it really boils down to is that Christianity, in its truest form, is a relationship and not a religion, and that relationship is something we all need in our life. That young man I spoke of earlier may be correct in saying that he doesn't need "religion" to get by in life. What he doesn't realize is that the void where he feels that he is missing out on something in life can only be filled by having a personal relationship with God through accepting Jesus Christ as his Savior from sin. He is missing out on a close, personal relationship with God that allows him to learn and grow in the fullness of life, and the satisfaction that he is in tune with God and is operating in God's perfect plan for his life. He is not missing out on a religion; he is missing out on a relationship.

Some people choose not to believe in Christianity, because they just can't see where you could ever get all the answers. But, when you realize that your answers have come from God, and that God is all-knowing, you realize that through communicating to God through Christ, you can receive all the answers that you need. The key is faith, believing that there actually is a God and believing that Jesus Christ is the Son of God and that we can achieve salvation through accepting him as our Savior. If you don't have faith and believe something can happen, then nothing will happen. But, if you do have faith and believe that something can happen, then something will happen. Your life will be forever changed. You will never be the same if you choose to believe the truth about Jesus Christ. The greatness of the God whom we serve is that he gives us the choice to live our lives as we wish. We can accept his plan for salvation through

Jesus Christ and spend eternity with him in heaven, or, we can reject his plan for salvation through Jesus Christ and spend eternity in damnation and Hell. It's really that simple.

I have heard people say that if God is such a great God, why would he send us to Hell if we don't live the way he wants us to? From that perspective it seems as though God could be cruel and mean. In their minds, they picture God blasting us with lightning bolts if we don't do as he says. This way of thinking couldn't be any further from the truth. It is not God's choice to send anyone to Hell. By giving us a chance to accept salvation through Jesus Christ, God gave us a way to keep from going to Hell. God placed the choice in the palms of our hands. Even though God wants all of us to live eternally in Heaven with him, God also graciously allows us to choose our own direction in life. It's up to us to choose Jesus Christ as our Savior if we wish to keep ourselves from going to Hell. There are only two possible places for us to go when this life is over, Heaven or Hell. The Bible clearly states that no man shall come to our Father God in Heaven, except for those who come by the name of Jesus Christ. If you don't end up going to Heaven, there is only one other place for you to go. Personally, I don't understand how any "religion" could disregard a statement that is so true and so vital. I hope the choice you make is a good decision. After all, the choice is yours to make.

I mentioned earlier that all we have to do is follow God's direction through Jesus and be obedient to that direction and God's word to us in the Bible, and we would never lose our salvation again. I know that many people believe that we are capable of losing our salvation through sinning. Others believe that once you accept Jesus Christ as your Savior, you are relinquished from your past, present, and future sins and will always maintain your salvation no matter what happens throughout the rest of your life.

I was taught in my upbringing that a person is capable of

losing his or her salvation. However, through experiencing the awesome grace of God upon my life in the past three or four years, I have come to question how far a person really has to go in order to lose their salvation. In some of the more severe cases, I believe it is possible. There has to be a place at which a fine line can be drawn. This place lies somewhere within the true intentions of our heart. That is where I take my striving towards perfection in my walk with God seriously, but at the same time, I don't let the fact that I do screw up and fail God on occasion drive me out of my mind psychologically. Since we are human, we cannot help but make mistakes from time to time and God is well aware of this fact. But, I do believe that I could possibly be playing around with my salvation if I do not ask God's forgiveness once again immediately after my screw up and go back to striving toward being the person whom God wants me to be.

I guess I look at it as if I were on top of a skyscraper and I know I shouldn't be getting too close to the edge of the building. I don't think it is the wisest thing to be pretending that I might jump off the side and plunge to certain death if I know that the possibility is there that I may actually lose my balance and fall. But then, there have been many times when I have slipped and fallen and God has reached out and caught me. Then he patiently and carefully brought me back closer to him. I just don't want to be like the child who kept jumping, expecting his father to catch him, until one day his father wasn't there to catch him because his father had realized his child's true intentions were not in serving his father, but his true intentions were in living a life of sin.

What do you think? Do you believe a person is truly capable of losing his or her salvation? I would like to point out a Scripture that tells us it is possible for us to lose our salvation. The determining factor as to whether or not we actually can lose our salvation is dependent upon a decision that we choose to make. This Scripture is Hebrews 10:26, 27, which states, "For if we sin willfully after that we have received the knowledge of the truth, there remaineth no more sacrifice for sins, but a certain fearful looking for of judgment and fiery indignation, which shall devour the adversaries."

This is basically saying that if we sin willfully after receiving our salvation, then we are willfully casting away our salvation. This doesn't mean that once you have cast away your salvation there is no way you can ever receive your salvation again. All you have to do is ask God's forgiveness and you will once again receive your salvation as long as you are sincere about your repentance. So the next time you may be wondering about your salvation, search your heart to find out what your true intentions are. If your true intentions reveal to you that you are on the right course, keep up the faith and keep moving forward in Jesus Christ. If your true intentions reveal to you that you have fallen into a selfish sinful nature, be quick to repent and ask God for forgiveness once again through Jesus Christ. Obtaining salvation does not come by asking God's forgiveness and then disregarding everything God tells you for the remainder of your life. Obtaining salvation comes from asking God's forgiveness and remaining committed and devoted to God throughout the remainder of your life. So the next time you may be questioning your salvation, ask yourself this question. What are my true intentions?

Philippians 4:7–9

And the peace of God, which passeth all understanding, shall keep your hearts and minds through Christ Jesus. Finally, brethren, whatsoever things are true, honest, just, pure, lovely, and of good report; if there be any virtue, and if there be any praise, think on these things. Those things, which ye have both learned, and received, and heard, and seen in me, do: and the God of peace shall be with you.

2 Corinthians 13:5

Examine yourselves, whether ye be in the faith; prove your own selves. Know ye not your own selves, how that Jesus Christ is in you, except ye be reprobates?

Matthew 26:41

Watch and pray, that ye enter not into temptation: the spirit indeed is willing, but the flesh is weak.

Galatians 3:22–29

But the scripture hath concluded all under sin, that the promise by faith of Jesus Christ might be given to them that believe. But before faith came, we were kept under the law, shut up unto the faith which should afterwards be revealed. Wherefore the law was our schoolmaster to bring us unto Christ, that we might be justified by faith. But after that faith is come, we are no longer under a schoolmaster. For ye are all the children of God by faith in Christ Jesus. For as many of you as have been baptized into Christ have put on Christ. There is neither Jew nor Greek, there is neither bond nor free, there is neither male nor female; for ye are all one in Christ Jesus. And if ye be Christ's, then are ye Abraham's seed, and heirs according to the promise.

Galatians 5:16–26

This I say then, Walk in the Spirit, and ye shall not fulfill the lust of the flesh. For the flesh lusteth against the Spirit, and the Spirit against the flesh: and these are contrary the one to the other: so that ye cannot do the things that ye would. But if ye be led of the Spirit, ye are not under the law. Now the works of the flesh are manifest, which are these: adultery, fornication, uncleanness, lasciviousness, idolatry, witchcraft, hatred, variance, emulations, wrath, strife, seditions, heresies, envyings, murders, drunkenness, revellings, and such like, of the which I tell you before, as I have also told you in time past, that they which do such things shall not inherit the kingdom of God. But the fruit of the Spirit is love, joy, peace, longsuffering, gentleness, goodness, faith, meekness, temperance: against such there is no law. And they that are Christ's have crucified the flesh with the affections and lusts. If we live in the Spirit, let us also walk in the Spirit. Let us not be desirous of vain glory, provoking one another, envying one another.

James 1:12–27

Blessed is the man that endureth temptation: for when he is tried, he shall receive the crown of life, which the Lord hath promised to them that love him. Let no man say when he is tempted, I am tempted of God: for God cannot be tempted with evil, neither tempteth he any man: But every man is tempted, when he is drawn away of his own lust, and enticed. Then when lust hath conceived, it bringeth forth sin: and sin, when it is finished, bringeth forth death. Do not err, my beloved brethren. Every good gift and every perfect gift is from above, and cometh down from the Father of lights, with whom is no variableness, neither shadow of turning. Of his own will begat he us with the word of truth, we should be a kind of firstfruits of his creatures. Wherefore, my beloved brethren, let every man be swift to hear, slow to speak, slow to wrath: For the wrath of man worketh not the righteousness of God. Wherefore lay apart all filthiness and superfluity of naughtiness, and receive with meekness the engrafted word, which is able to save your souls. But be ye doers of the word, and not hearers only, deceiving your own selves. For if any be a hearer of the word, and not a doer, he is like unto a man beholding his natural face in a glass: For he beholdeth himself, and goeth his way, and straightway forgetteth what manner of man he was.

But whoso looketh into the perfect law of liberty, and continueth therein, he being not a forgetful hearer, but a doer of the work, this man shall be blessed in his deed. If any man among you seem to be religious, and bridleth not his tongue, but deceiveth his own heart, this man's religion is vain. Pure religion and undefiled before God and the Father is this, To visit the fatherless and widows in their affliction, and to keep himself unspotted from the world.

Matthew 7:1–27

Judge not, that ye be not judged. For with what judgment ye judge, ye shall be judged: and with what measure ye mete, it shall be measured to you again. And why beholdest thou the mote that is in thy brother's eye, but considerest not the beam that is in thine own eye? Or how wilt thou say to thy brother, Let me pull out the mote out of thine eye; and, behold, a beam is in thine own eye? Thou hypocrite, first cast out the beam out of thine own eye; and then shalt thou see clearly to cast out the mote out of thy brother's eye. Give not that which is holy unto the dogs, neither cast ye your pearls before swine, lest they trample them under their feet, and turn again and rend you. Ask, and it shall be given you; seek, and ye shall find; knock, and it shall be opened unto you: For every one that asketh receiveth; and he that seeketh findeth; and to him that knocketh it shall be opened. Or what man is there of you, whom if his son asked bread, will he give him a stone? Or if he ask a fish, will he give him a serpent? If ye then, being evil, know how to give good gifts unto your children, how much more shall your Father which is in heaven given good things to them that ask him? Therefore all things whatsoever ye would that men should do to you, do ye even so to them: for this is the law and the prophets. Enter ye in at the strait gate: for wide is the gate, and broad is the way, that leadeth to destruction, and many there be which go in thereat: Because strait is the gate, and narrow is the way, which leadeth unto life, and few there be that find it.

Beware of false prophets, which come to you in sheep's

clothing, but inwardly they are ravening wolves. Ye shall know them by their fruits. Do men gather grapes of thorns, or figs of thistles? Even so every good tree bringeth forth good fruit; but a corrupt tree bringeth forth evil fruit. A good tree cannot bring forth evil fruit, neither can a corrupt tree bring forth good fruit. Every tree that bringeth not forth good fruit is hewn down, and cast into the fire. Wherefore by their fruits ye shall know them.

Not every one that saith unto me, Lord, Lord, shall enter into the kingdom of heaven; but he that doeth the will of my Father which is in heaven. Many will say to me in that day, Lord, Lord, have we not prophesied in thy name? And in thy name have cast out devils? And in thy name done many wonderful works? And then will I profess unto them, I never knew you: depart from me, ye that work iniquity. Therefore whosoever heareth these sayings of mine, and doeth them, I will liken him unto a wise man, which built his house upon a rock: And the rain descended, and the floods came, and the winds blew, and beat upon that house; and it fell not: for it was founded upon a rock. And every one that heareth these sayings of mine, and doeth them not, shall be likened unto a foolish man, which built his house upon the sand: And the rain descended, and the floods came, and the winds blew, and beat upon that house; and it fell: and great was the fall of it.

1 Corinthians 15:22

For as in Adam all die, even so in Christ shall all be made alive.

John 14:6

Jesus saith unto him, I am the way, the truth, and the life: no man cometh unto the Father, but by me.

Behold, I stand at the door, and knock: if any man hear my voice, and open the door, I will come in to him, and will sup with him, and he with me. To him that overcometh will I grant to sit with me in my throne, even as I also overcame, and am set down with my Father in his throne.

Six

Integrity

The just man walketh in his integrity: his children are blessed after him.

—Proverbs 20:7

If I could encourage you in any area of your life, I would choose to encourage you to remain steadfast in your devotion to God. God doesn't always give us the answers for all of our questions in life. Sometimes he realizes that we are better off not knowing certain things. Just because God doesn't reveal everything to us that we may think we need to know, doesn't mean we should question him or put conditions on serving him. Sometimes we just need to watch the water flow under the bridge and let it go downstream. Sometimes we just need to stand tall in the face of adversity and keep our feet firmly planted while trusting in the strength of a mighty God. Sometimes all we need is integrity.

Integrity is something that is gained through experience. It is a combination of many different characteristics. A person doesn't just wake up one day and automatically have integrity. Gaining integrity takes an experience with something in order to build a foundation on which you can make a stand for that which you believe in. Gaining integrity takes an experience with God. Once we experience the awesomeness of God and the grace he has extended to us, a desire is born inside of us to live our lives in a manner that would be pleasing to him. This is not something that can be accomplished as easily as turning on a light switch. It is something that we learn over time through various experiences and circumstances in our lives. If it is our true desire to serve God, we must remain devoted to him in our walk through life. Over time we will begin to develop a set of standards by which we live our life. We will become disciplined in our lifestyle as we learn and grow in the integrity of God.

Integrity involves things such as maintaining a set of priorities upon which we build our whole lives around. Priorities, such as putting God first in every facet of our lives or putting the needs of our spouse or children first instead of our own desires. Some people think of integrity as something that makes them better than other people. They don't know what the true meaning of integrity is, because they are operating out of pride and trying to stick their noses into the air. A person who has integrity is a person who is humble in spirit and takes into consideration the thoughts and concerns of others. Integrity never places anyone above any other person. However, integrity does place you above sin. Integrity involves being obedient to God. Doing things for God out of love and reverence toward him rather than waiting until we are forced into a corner. Integrity involves things such as being responsible or keeping your word, especially when it's a major sacrifice to do so.

A person who has integrity is one who is an honest, truthful, down-to-earth, genuine friend. They are people who know the true value of life. They are people who know that true friendship is an investment that involves taking the time to deposit love and care into it. They are people who accept other people as they are without putting conditions on anything. They realize that even though someone may seem weird and different, he or she should not be considered an outcast. That person might not be so weird and different if others would take the time to show some concern and care.

People who have integrity realize that they are able to have an impact on the world around them through the choices that they make in daily situations and circumstances. They realize the importance of doing or saying the right thing and they strive to keep God first in their decision-making process. Time for a reality check. Is what you are about to say or do going to accomplish anything for the kingdom of God? In other words, is it worth saying or doing at all? If we are not truly putting God first in our decision-making, how can we even dare to think we can make the right decisions? Who is really in control? It's your choice. It's your life.

Life doesn't just happen to people. You can make a difference through choices that you make every day. You do have a choice and the choice you make in life reflects who you are and what you really believe in. The old saying still holds true that our actions speak louder than our words do. The key is to keep our eyes focused on Jesus Christ. Jesus was our example of how we should live our lives and how we are called to live by his example. In Matthew 5:48, Jesus Christ tells us to "be perfect, even as your Father which is in heaven is perfect." But we are only human. How can we be perfect? Romans 5:19 states that "for as by one man's (Adam's) disobedience many were made sinners, so by the obedience of one (Jesus Christ) shall many be made righteous." 1 John 3:5, 6 also says "and ye know that he (Jesus Christ) was manifested to take away our sins; and in him is no sin. Whosoever abideth in him sinneth not." So what do we have now? We know that we are made righteous through Jesus Christ and that if we abide in Him that we will not sin. So what exactly does abiding in Jesus Christ mean? The definition of "abide" is to stand fast, to remain, or to go on being. It is to stay, reside, await, submit to, or put up with. It is also to live up to a promise or agreement or to submit to and carry out a rule or decision. I would like to also key in on the word "submit." Many people perceive the word "submit" as an authoritative word, which demands compliance when in all reality it is not. The true definition of submission is a giving of oneself to another out of love towards the other. So now we know that if we give of ourselves out of love for God and stand fast, remaining devoted to him and residing in his presence, we are abiding in him. So how do we know that he is abiding in us? In John 14:21, Jesus said, "he that hath my commandments, and keepeth them, he it is that loveth me: and he that loveth me shall be loved of my father, and I will love him, and will manifest myself to him." Now we know that if we choose to abide in Jesus, he will abide in us. If this relationship is taking place, we will receive the instruction we need from God to keep ourselves from sinning.

We may not be able to be perfect because of our old human nature, but we can be perfect by confiding in God. God is our best friend. The Bible tells us in 1 Thessalonians 5:17 to "pray without ceasing." Prayer is not just asking God to do something. Prayer is conversation with God. Prayer without ceasing is constantly including God in our thought patterns just like a conversation with our best friend. God is our best friend. He can't let us down. He won't let us down. How could we not confide in and share our life with God? Christianity is a relationship with God. You get out of a relationship what you put into a relationship. If you give him thirty percent of yourself, you won't get much in return. But, if you give him one hundred percent of yourself, you will receive rewards far greater than you could ever gain in this world. People who have integrity choose to stay in tune with God because they realize that without God they are only opening themselves up to sin. Just as 1 John 3:6 states that "whosoever abideth in him (Jesus Christ) sinneth not," it also goes on to say that "whosoever sinneth hath not seen him, neither know him."

In other words, if we abide in Jesus Christ, we are capable of keeping ourselves from sinning. On the other hand, if we do not abide in Jesus Christ, we are not capable of keeping ourselves from sinning. True integrity comes from communion with Jesus Christ. Communion is an intimate way of communicating with one another. This is when true Christianity becomes a relationship and not a religion. When we abide in Jesus Christ and he abides in us, we are operating in the formula that keeps us from sinning.

This is a formula that takes into consideration the true meaning of the words "abide" and "submit." By applying the true definitions of "abide" and "submit" to 1 John 3:6 and 1 Thessalonians 5:17, we come up with the following: whosoever would totally commit themselves to God out of love for God, prioritizing their life around him in every way imaginable while constantly communicating with him in order to keep themselves or their circumstances from having any effect on their decisionmaking process is able to keep themselves from sin. Mark 7:15 states that "There is nothing from without man, that entering into him can defile him: but the things which come out of him, those are they that defile the man." Our circumstances cannot force us to sin, but if we allow our circumstances to govern our response when we have not been communicating with Jesus Christ, we are almost certain to react to our situation in a sinful manner. However, if we have been spending time in communication with Jesus Christ and our priorities are right, we are certain to react to our situation in an appropriate manner. A person with integrity realizes the importance of this fact and strives daily to read his or her Bible and spend time in prayer.

A person with integrity has faith in God's word. A person with integrity has the kind of faith that is spoken of in Philippians 1:6, which states that "being confident of this very thing, that he which hath begun a good work in you will perform it until the day of Jesus Christ." Integrity is the foundation on which faith is built. Integrity is a stubborn kind of faith. It involves taking a stand for what you believe in. Integrity is standing tall and strong when everything else around you is telling you to tuck your tail between your legs and run away. In the Bible, Job had the integrity it took when he lost all that he had, but still remained devoted to God. Shadrach, Meshach, and Abednego had the integrity it took when King Nebuchadnezzar tried to get them to bow down to a false god. Noah had the integrity that it took when all the people ridiculed him for believing that God wanted him to build an ark. Integrity along with faith produces the stamina it takes to endure all of the challenges of life no matter how great they are. When you have integrity and faith working together, you can say, "I don't care what anyone else says because I know what God's word says." You can say, "I will not compromise the word of God for any reason," or, "I don't have to conform to the way this world thinks and operates." You can also say, "I will settle for nothing less than what God would have me do." Integrity dares to be different.

A person with integrity develops confidence from spending time with God. Time for another reality check. Take a step back. Look at that person in the mirror. Is that person confident or is that person confused? Confusion comes from not spending time in prayer or reading the Bible. Being uncertain of what you should do in any given situation or being uncertain of what God wants you to do with your life is proof enough to show you that you have not been spending time alone consulting God. First Corinthians 14:33 says that God is not the author of confusion, but of peace. A person with integrity is never confused because he or she spends time with God daily.

A person with integrity seeks wise counsel. Proverbs 12:15 states, "The way of a fool is right in his own eyes: but he that hearkeneth unto counsel is wise." Proverbs 19:20 states, "Hear counsel, and receive instruction, that thou mayest be wise in thy latter end." A person with integrity takes into consideration the knowledge and wisdom that other people have. I remember when I was in my high school history class and we were studying Adolf Hitler. Our history book had a picture of Hitler and below it was a caption stating a famous quote from George Santayana. It read, "Those who fail to remember the past are destined to repeat it." Adolf Hitler is certainly not one who deserves to be exalted, but there is a lot of truth to what Santayana said. A person with integrity not only learns from his own experience, a person with integrity learns from the experience of others in order to be prepared should a similar circumstance arise in his or her own life. One of the biggest reasons God gave us the Bible is so we can learn from the experiences of others. How could we disregard something so important and vital to life? A person with integrity realizes the value of God's word and seeks the knowledge and wisdom that it has to offer.

Proverbs 8:34, 35: "Blessed is the man that heareth me, watching daily at my gates, waiting at the posts of my doors. For whoso findeth me findeth life, and shall obtain favour of the LORD."

A person with integrity receives reassurance from God. Sometimes when you are in tune with God, he will give you the same thing that he gives to someone else. This is one way that he lets us know that we are on the right track. My wife and I were driving home from vacation one day when God began to speak to my heart. God placed on my heart the story of the prodigal son and he was focusing on the forgiveness and love that the father gave when his son had returned home. I began to dwell on the subject. At the time I was involved in the men's ministry at our church and I thought that God was giving me something that he wanted me to use in our next meeting. I began to think about times in the past when I had seen people hold grudges against their brothers in Christ because of something petty that happened between the two of them. One of them eventually came to his senses and apologized, but the other person never truly forgave him. It was all just an act. I thought about other people who rather than forgive and forget, said I told you so. Those situations weren't true forgiveness, but those people claimed to be Christians. When we got home from vacation and went to church the next Sunday, I listened to our pastor preach on the exact same message that God put on my heart. How about that for a surprise? I thought, *God, how am I supposed to use what you're giving me if you just gave the same thing to our pastor and he's already used it.* But then that just reassured me that I was on the right track.

A person with integrity is an excellent witness for God. My wife and I went canoeing one summer day, and as we were going downstream, we came upon a tree that was growing sideways out of the bank of the river. It had to be leaning at least a fifty- or sixty-degree angle. The branches extended out to where they were just above the water. It was sure a silly looking tree. I looked to go around the tree, but the water was too shallow on that side of the river. There was just the narrowest of gaps where we could duck down and pass underneath the tree, so I told my wife to prepare herself because that was the only way we could pass. She began to talk about how the tree was sideways and expressed her concern that if we passed underneath it, that it might fall on us. I had to reassure her that the tree looked very healthy and secure and that if it had been going to fall over, it probably would have done that a long time ago. We both ducked down, passed safely under the tree, and went on our way.

It was later on that God showed me a similarity between that tree and a good Christian witness. He brought to mind an old hymn that says, "Just like the tree that's planted by the water, I shall not be moved." A good Christian witness is just like that tree, planted firmly on the foundation of Christ and receiving living water that flows from God's word. As we build our foundation on Christ, this allows us to grow into being what God wants us to be. We may grow sideways and look a little funny, but that only causes the world to take notice and examine us a little closer. It also gives us an opportunity to witness to the world the faith that we hold in our heart.

1 Peter 2:9: "But ye are a chosen generation, a royal priesthood, an holy nation, a peculiar people; that ye should shew forth the praises of him who hath called you out of darkness into his marvelous light."

People with integrity keep themselves under the microscope. They examine their own hearts to see what is inside and make the changes necessary in order to go in the direction God would have them go. For the measure of a person is not the decisions he or she makes when in the spotlight. The measure of a person involves the decisions he makes when there is nobody around to see or to know except himself and God.

Psalms 19:14

Let the words of my mouth, and the meditation of my heart, be acceptable in thy sight, O LORD, my strength, and my redeemer.

Hebrews 10:23

Let us hold fast the profession of our faith without wavering: for he is faithful that promised.

Seven
Happiness, Peace, and Contentment

God wants us to be happy and content with our lives. If we spend all of our time worrying about unachieved goals, we will be consumed by our worries and they will start controlling our lives. We slowly start becoming more bitter and envious toward those people who have more things than we have. In any event, we become slaves to the things of this world. What does it matter if our neighbor has the nicest house and the nicest car on the block? Sure, I like nice things too, but let's not let them control our lives. If we settle down and rest in the presence of God, we will find that our salvation through Christ means more to us than all of those things. Our priorities start to change and all of a sudden those things don't matter anymore. We need to learn to be content with what God has blessed us with already and trust that if God has brought us this far in our lives, he will surely take us farther.

In order for us to achieve more of God's blessings in life, we must go through a test of commitment and faith in God. If we pass the test, God blesses us further in life because we have proven that we are worthy of his blessing. If we do not pass the test, God will take the blessing away from us until we can be responsible enough to be blessed and still keep God first in our lives. God does not want anything to intervene in his relationship with us. As long as we keep God first and are thankful for what he has given to us, he will continue to bless us more. So all we really have to do is follow God and enjoy life.

1 John 2:15–17

Love not the world, neither the things that are in the world. If any man love the world, the love of the Father is not in him. For all that is in the world, the lust of the flesh, and the lust of the eyes, and the pride of life, is not of the Father, but is of the world. And the world passeth away, and the lust thereof: but he that doeth the will of God abideth for ever.

Mark 4:19

And the cares of this world, and the deceitfulness of riches, and the lusts of other things entering in, choke the word, and it becometh unfruitful.

Titus 2:11–14

For the grace of God that bringeth salvation hath appeared to all men, teaching us that, denying ungodliness and worldly lusts, we should live soberly, righteously, and godly, in this present world; looking for that blessed hope, and the glorious appearing of the great God and our Savior Jesus Christ; who gave himself for us, that he might redeem us from all iniquity, and purify unto himself a peculiar people, zealous of good works.

God wants us to be a witness to other people in everything we do. We cannot do this if we are all caught up in our own concerns. Someone might be watching you and find that you are just as worried about life as they are. They may think that you are no more better off than they are. Therefore, through their eyes, your Christian life has nothing to offer them.

Think about it for a minute. Everyone in this world is

searching for happiness, peace, and contentment. The problem is that most people believe the way to achieve those goals is through obtaining bigger and better things in life. They keep finding something nicer than that which they have, and the things they have are no longer as exciting as when they first received them. Most people do not know how to be content with what they have. If they see that you have the same or less than they do, and are happier with your life than they are with theirs, then they start wondering why you are happy. They start watching you and trying to figure out what you have that they don't have. Once they find that God is the reason you are happy with your life, they may become more open to you and God. This is where God can work through you as an effective witness for him.

Being an effective witness for God does not require bothering people and pushing tracts at them all of the time. If anything, this tends to turn most people off and they will not want to listen to what you have to say. All you really have to do is wait until people start coming to you and asking you questions so they can find out what makes you tick. Then you can pray that God gives you the right words to say, and he will do just that. You don't have to fit in with the crowd. Sooner or later the crowd will be watching you, trying to figure you out. They will realize that they rely on each other and they will wonder why you don't have to rely on them. Once they find out that only God can give them true happiness, they will begin to desire God in their hearts. The plan is very simple. All you have to do is follow God and his commandments, be happy and content with your life, and you will be an excellent witness for God.

Hebrews 13:5, 6

Let your conversation be without covetousness; and be content with such things as ye have; for he hath said, I will never leave

80

thee, nor forsake thee. So that we may boldly say, The Lord is my helper, and I will not fear what man shall do unto me.

Matthew 11:28–30

Come unto me all ye that labor and are heavy laden, and I will give you rest. Take my yoke upon you, and learn of me; for I am meek and lowly in heart: and ye shall find rest unto your souls. For my yoke is easy, and my burden is light.

Eight
The Challenge

If I were to summarize what this book is about, I would say that it is a book for people who desire to seek after God's will for their life and could use a little encouragement. I might also say that it is a book that challenges you to take a good hard look at who you are and whether or not you are a person who might need to look at life from a different perspective. Or, I might say that it is a book that could be used to show people who aren't Christians what true Christianity is, as opposed to someone who claims to be a Christian, when in all reality he or she probably isn't. To those types of people, I would like to apologize for all the times I may have acted hypocritically in my Christian walk.

I would also like to encourage you to know that if God can help me change my life through accepting His son Jesus Christ as my Savior and Redeemer from sin, then God can do the same for you. There is only one way to God and that is through the sacrificial blood of Jesus Christ as the payment for our sin, asking God to forgive us and allowing Jesus Christ to come into our heart and cleanse us from sin. There is no other way back to God but through the saving grace of Jesus christ. No person can save you. No religion can save you. No church can save you. No good deeds can save you. Nothing, absolutely nothing can save you from the clutches of sin and eternal damnation except for the blood of Jesus Christ.

Once you have accepted Jesus Christ as your Savior, the best thing you can do is live what you believe in. Instead of putting your money where your mouth is, put your life where your mouth is. There are already enough hypocrites in this world, and we surely don't need any more of them. However, we sure could use a lot more good, honest, down-to-earth true Christians. Accepting Jesus Christ as our Savior from sin is the best thing that could happen to our lives. The best thing that we could do after that is to devote our life to being the truest Christians we can be. After all, a true Christian doesn't just tell people about Jesus Christ; a true Christian backs what he or she says by their actions of true love, care, and concern for the welfare of others.

There is one other thing I think about when I consider summarizing what this book is about. I am reminded of a song that was written by Raymond McDonald and Bobby McDonald. They are members of the blues band Sleepy Ray and the Mighty Blood, which is the best thing to happen to music since Russ Taff. They sing a song called "Ain't Talkin' 'bout it." The following words are the lyrics to that song:

I ain't talkin' 'bout women
Or the things that they do.
I ain't talkin' 'bout religion
Ain't pointing the finger at you.
I ain't talkin' 'bout no
bleedin' hearts.
I'm just talkin' 'bout truth.

I ain't talkin' 'bout gamblin'
Or whether you lose or you win.
I ain't talkin' 'bout ramblin'
Or anywhere that you've been.
I ain't talkin' 'bout makin' love
I'm just talkin' 'bout Him.

That kind of life had a hold on me
But now I ain't the same.
'Cause there's a kind of love
That'll set you free
If you'll just believe in His name.

I ain't talkin' 'bout cheatin'
Or runnin' 'round on my wife.
I ain't talkin' 'bout drinkin'
Or gettin' cut with no knife.
I ain't talkin' 'bout dying young
I'm just talkin' 'bout life.

I ain't talkin' 'bout floodin'
How high the water done fell.
I ain't talkin' 'bout muggin'
Or spendin' the night in no jail.
I ain't talkin' 'bout flashy cars
I'm just talkin' 'bout
Jesus, baby, Jesus.

I don't think you could sum up this book any better than
that. The Bible says that Jesus is the way, the truth, and the life,
and that no man can come to God but by the name of Jesus
Christ. I would like to encourage you all to accept Jesus Christ
as your Savior if you haven't already done so. I would also like
to challenge you to devote your life to whatever God has in
store for you. If you do so, you will never regret it. It's the
greatest thing that could ever happen to anyone. If you have
never accepted Jesus Christ as your Savior and you aren't sure
how to do so, it is really very simple. All you have to do is pray
the following prayer, and be honest and truthful in your intentions to accept Jesus Christ as your Savior. God will know if

you are honest and truthful in your intentions or not. Because, after all, God knows the intentions of our heart better than we know them.

The Prayer of Salvation

Dear God,

I realize that all men are born into sin in this world and that sin separates me from you. I believe that Jesus christ is the Son of God and that Jesus came into this world to live a life without sin, and that He gave His life when He died on the cross as the perfect sacrifice for my sin. Jesus Christ paid the penalty for all of my sins, and I now accept Him as my Lord and Savior. I ask for forgiveness for all of the sins that I have committed in my life. I thank you for your grace and mercy, which allows me to come to you through the blood Jesus shed when He died for me. I thank you for giving me this gift of eternal life and I now devote my life to your will. May my life now be an example of the way a true Christian should live. I realize that I need to learn and grow in my Christian walk and I vow this day to read your word and to spend time with you regularly in prayer. I pray this prayer to you this day, Father God, in all honesty and sincerity, and I pray this prayer in Jesus' name. Amen.

If you prayed that prayer and sincerely meant it, you will feel a change take place on the inside of you. You will feel the awesome power of Jesus Christ cleansing you from all of your sins. From now on, your life will never be the same. It will be greater than you ever dreamed possible as long as you stay devoted to God. Congratulations, and welcome to the Kingdom of God! May all you do from this day on be to the glory of God. May all your footsteps be ordered of God as you experience the wonderful joy of living for Him. May you also receive God's richest blessings upon your life.

Some people think that it would be too difficult for them to live a Christian life. There are many people in this world who believe this lie. They start thinking about everything in their lives that they would have to give up. They also think that it is a major struggle and there are too many burdens on Christians. If I had to live up to how the world thinks a Christian should act, I might have felt the same way as these people. It would seem impossible. This makes me glad that I know that even though God wants us to follow his commandments, he also knows we are only human, and prone to fail at times. The only one who is required to be perfect is God. His mercy is what allows us to have the strength we need to live our Christian life.

God doesn't want us to be perfect when we accept him. He just wants us to get started in the right direction. Then he can begin to work on us and filter out the bad things in our lives. Eventually, we will be living our lives the way God wants us to live. Living a Christian life is not hard to do at all. All we are required to do is what God tells us to do. God would never tell us to do anything we couldn't handle. If it seems to be a task that is too great for you, remember that God will be right there with you to help you accomplish your goal. God will give us the strength we need to make it through any struggle. All we have to do is ask for his help. I am so thankful that we serve a God with so much mercy, understanding, patience, and love. Where would we be without him?

Matthew 12:28–30

Come unto me, all ye that labour and are heavy laden, and I will give you rest. Take my yoke upon you, and learn of me; for I am meek and lowly in heart: and ye shall find rest unto your souls. For my yoke is easy, and my burden is light.

Romans 10:9, 10

That if thou shalt confess with thy mouth the Lord Jesus, and shalt believe in thine heart that God hath raised him from the dead, thou shalt be saved. For with the heart man believeth unto righteousness; and with the mouth confession is made unto salvation.

2 Timothy 4:7–8

I have fought a good fight, I have finished my course, I have kept the faith: Henceforth there is laid up for me a crown of righteousness, which the Lord, the righteous judge, shall give me at that day: and not to me only, but unto all them also that love his appearing.

John 3:16–21

For God so loved the world, that he gave his only begotten Son, that whosoever believeth in him should not perish, but have everlasting life. For God sent not his Son into the world to condemn the world; but that the world through him might be saved. He that believeth on him is not condemned: but he that believeth not is condemned already, because he hath not believed in the name of the only begotten Son of God. And this is the condemnation, that light is come into the world, and men loved darkness rather than light, because their deeds were evil. For every one that doeth evil hateth the light, neither cometh to the light, lest his deeds should be reproved. But he that doeth truth cometh to the light, that his deeds may be made manifest, that they are wrought in God.

2 Chronicles 7:14

If my people, which are called by my name, shall humble themselves, and pray, and seek my face, and turn from their wicked ways; then will I hear from heaven, and will forgive their sin, and will heal their land.

Psalms 86:5

For thou, Lord, art good, and ready to forgive; and plenteous in mercy unto all them that call upon thee.

1 John 1:9

If we confess our sins, he is faithful and just to forgive us our sins, and to cleanse us from all unrighteousness.

Nine
The Bible, It's Our Responsibility

A Christian walk is like an automobile. You have to keep investing in maintenance or it will deteriorate and fall apart. Colossians chapter three tells us about how we should approach situations and relationships. Nowhere is this more important than in our Christian walk. If we react correctly in some situations and react incorrectly in other situations, then we are sending mixed signals to other people, which only results in confusion. A Christian walk requires a strong foundation in which to build upon. One that is constant, secure, and has balance. Taking the time to read the Bible to learn how to respond to any given situation or relationship helps us to build a strong foundation for our Christian walk. Having that stability only allows for greater strides to be taken in our Christian walk in the future. One thing that we need to keep in mind is that, just like that automobile, we get out of our Christian walk what we put into it.

With life comes learning and the things we learn in life all add to our growth as individuals. Sometimes we learn through our own experience. Sometimes we learn through the experiences of others. One thing is for sure, it is easier to learn from someone else's experience than it is to have to go through what they did in order to learn the same thing. What better place is there to learn than in the Bible? The Bible offers many stories and lessons from which we can learn through the experiences of others. All we have to do is read it.

There is a billboard I have driven past many times that I find to be amusing, but truthful. It states, "If God wrote an editorial in the local newspaper, you would read it, wouldn't you?" The picture on the billboard shows our local newspaper with a Bible lying on top of it. The message is pretty simple. God doesn't have to write an article in the local newspaper because God has already revealed to us everything we need to know in the Bible. It's up to us to read it and put it into effect in our life. However, many people just do not choose to do this. In fact, most people choose to find all kinds of excuses as to why they can't do this one simple thing. There are either too many "thees" and "thous" in the Bible, or people say they just don't have the time to read it.

Wait a minute. We have time to fit everything else into our life. What about one chapter, or even one verse of Scripture? Why would anyone blow off something that holds so many answers about life within its pages. If there is something you don't understand, just move on until you find something that you do understand. Chances are that is the part of the Bible you should probably be reading anyway. There are many things in the Bible that anyone can understand. Once you have learned the little things, you find yourself picking up on bigger things. You begin to learn and grow in the knowledge of God and the understanding of life. You begin to learn the wisdom of great men and how God uses common simple people to do great things for him. You begin to grow in faith through experiencing the faith of others.

The Bible begins to come alive and real inside you, and starts to feed your soul with fire and faith. You begin to remember certain Scriptures when you need them, and God's word becomes the major driving force behind your life. It lifts you up when you are down. It carries you through when you can't carry on. It gives you comfort in times of sorrow. It gives you joy when you have the blues. It gives you strength when you are at your weakest. It helps you relax when you are stressed out. It gives you rest when you are tired. It gives you encouragement when you are discouraged. It gives you confidence when you feel as if you just can't do anything right. The Bible can help you accomplish many things in life, but it doesn't help you if you don't read it and don't have the faith to believe in what it says. A good example of this is the time that my wife and I set aside for family devotions.

One of the things I have grown to appreciate from marriage is the time that my wife and I have spent together in our devotions. When we first started our devotion time, I felt very uncomfortable. My family had never done anything like this as a family. I was used to spending time reading the word by myself. I felt a little intimidated by the idea. I was afraid that my wife might expect me to be this know-it-all/prayer warrior/perfect example of a Godly leader. I was afraid if she didn't see this in me that she might think less of me or make fun of me.

I have always been the kind of person who is a thinker and a doer, but not always much of a talker. I can think about my feelings and what I want to say and then write it down on paper, but I don't always have an answer on the spur of a moment. Sometimes I know what I want to say, but I can't seem to find the right words to explain what I am thinking. I was afraid my wife might mistake this for being confused or not knowing anything. Also, I'm not one of those people who can start praying and really go to town and sound like I am preaching a sermon or something. My prayers have generally been short and to the point. God knows my heart and what I am trying to say or how much I mean what I am saying.

We decided to spend just a few minutes before bedtime reading a small passage out of a devotional book that my wife had purchased. Then we would say a short prayer and we would be finished. I think my wife may have been surprised at how short my prayer was. Her prayer was short also, but compared to mine, it seemed like about a half hour long. At times, all I could think of was, *My goodness, I hope she doesn't think I'm some bonehead.* It took me a while to open up and explain to her how awkward I felt. I was just glad that she was understanding and encouraging and didn't pick on me.

Having a devotion time has strengthened our marriage. We have drawn closer to each other. It helps keep our priorities straight. It keeps us in agreement on our goals. It also helps us encourage each other to be more open with each other. When we first started our devotion time, I wasn't sure if it was something I really wanted to do, but now I have learned to appreciate it as time well spent. Just a few minutes together in God's word can make a world of difference.

Part of growing up is accepting responsibility, so if you want to grow as an individual, you must be responsible enough to read the Bible and apply it to your life. The Bible is the key that unlocks the door to your dreams. With a key like that, all your dreams can come true. Let's be reasonable, though. Sometimes some of the dreams we think we have about life are really just lusts of our flesh and would not really make us happy at all. Our true dreams will bring us all the joys of life, and true happiness, peace and contentment. You couldn't ask for a happier life than when God is in control of your life. Just let go and give control of your life to God. Then, get ready for the greatest roller-coaster ride you have ever been on.

Romans 10:17

So then faith cometh by hearing, and hearing by the word of God.

Study to shew thyself approved unto God, a workman that needeth not to be ashamed, rightly dividing the word of truth. But shun profane and vain babblings: for they will increase unto more ungodliness.

Ten

Why Are We on This Planet?

Why are we on this planet? Have you figured it out yet? We are here to give our lives to God and do his will. Living for God is exciting and rewarding. You may not know what is going to happen next, but you can be sure God knows. Living for God is not hard. Sure, you will be tested and you will go through trying times in your life, but God will always be there with you. There will be times when you don't know what to do and all you have to rely on is God's word.

There was once a time when a man's word was worth his weight in silver. People lived by their word, and when they gave you their word, you knew they would not let you down. If this is true of mere mortal men, how much more can we rely on the word of God? God had already lived up to his word in our lives. He is just waiting for us to trust in him and be content, and allow him to work in our lives, and he will bless us beyond our deepest imaginations.

Life isn't about what we want; it is about what God wants. It's about helping people, showing God's love, being a true friend, and learning to listen and act when God tells us to do something. So relax, rest in God's arms, and enjoy the life he has given to you. May you all find happiness, joy, peace, contentment, and God's richest blessings in your life.

Isaiah 1:19, 20

If ye be willing and obedient, ye shall eat the good of the land: but if ye refuse and rebel, ye shall be devoured with the sword: for the mouth of the Lord hath spoken it.

Matthew 7:7–11

Ask, and it shall be given you; seek, and ye shall find; knock, and it shall be opened unto you: for everyone that asketh receiveth; and he that seeketh findeth; and to him that knocketh it shall be opened. Or what man is there of you, whom if his son asked bread, will he give him a stone? Of if he ask a fish, will he give him a serpent? If ye then, being evil, know how to give good gifts unto your children, how much more shall your Father which is in heaven give good things to them that ask him?

Psalms 23:1–6

The Lord is my shepherd; I shall not want. He maketh me to lie down in green pastures: he leadeth me beside the still waters. He restoreth my soul: he leadeth me in the paths of righteousness for his name's sake. Yea, though I walk through the valley of the shadow of death, I will fear no evil; for thou art with me; thy rod and thy staff they comfort me. Thou preparest a table before me in the presence of mine enemies: thou anointest my head with oil; my cup runneth over. Surely goodness and mercy shall follow me all the days of my life: and I will dwell in the house of the Lord for ever.

Finding God's Will for Your Life

When it is time for God's will to be done in your life, you will not have any doubt about what it is that God wants you to do. Sometimes it seems that God has forgotten us. We feel let down as we watch exciting things happen in the lives of other people, and it feels as if we are left standing still with nothing. This is a time when we need to wait on God's timing. God will never forget anyone. We may not yet be ready for what God has planned for our lives. God would never give us something that we are not ready for.

When I was about four years old and our family was on vacation, we stopped at a gas station to buy fuel. While the car was being filled, I went to use the rest room. On my way back, I noticed that the car was gone. *Oh, no,* I thought. *What am I going to do? They have forgotten me and are driving down the highway, and here I am stuck in the middle of nowhere.* I stood there afraid and confused for a while. Then, one of my sisters walked around the corner of the building and told me that everyone had been waiting for me to come back to the car. A feeling of relief came over me the moment I saw her. All they had done was drive around to the side of the gas station so somebody else could use the gas pump. They finally decided to send my sister to see what was taking me so long.

Sometimes it may seem as if you are just standing around and nothing is happening. If you watch closely, you will notice that you are learning more about how God works by seeing him work in the lives of the other people. It may seem as though God isn't doing anything in your life, but he really is at work. God is just waiting around the corner, and when it is time for you to do his will, he will walk around the corner, take you by the hand, and lead you to where he wants you to go. So be patient, wait on God's timing, and everything will work out just as it should.

Proverbs 8:34, 35

Blessed is the man that heareth me, watching daily at my gates, waiting at the posts of my door. For whoso findeth me findeth life, and shall obtain favour of the Lord.

Proverbs 3:5, 6

Trust in the Lord with all thine heart: and lean not unto thine own understanding, in all thy ways acknowledge him, and he shall direct thy paths.

Psalms 40:1, 2

I waited patiently for the Lord; and he inclined unto me, and heard my cry. He brought me up also out of an horrible pit, out of the miry clay, and set my feet upon a rock, and established my goings.

One thing that God likes to do is to work in areas of our lives in which we have very little knowledge of how to do what he wants done. Take this book, for example. One of the classes that I disliked the most in high school was my English class. I had absolutely no desire to do any more work than it took to obtain a passing grade. If you had told any of my high school classmates that I would eventually be the author of a book, they all would have laughed uproariously.

The reason God uses us the most in areas where we have little knowledge is that he can tell us what he wants done and we will do what he says without questioning him. If I had been an English major in college, I might have done things differently. I might have been working on other projects and felt that there would not be enough time for me to work on this book. God likes to work with our weaker points and make us stronger so we are able to face our next challenge in life. That makes life exciting because it makes you wonder what will happen next. In any event, whatever challenges you face, God will be there to help you through it. So sit back, relax, enjoy the ride, and let God direct you where he wants you to go in life.

Psalms 119:105

Thy word is a lamp unto my feet, and a light unto my path.

Psalms 73:24

Thou shalt guide me with thy counsel, and afterward receive me to glory.

Psalms 48:14

For this is our God for ever and ever: he will be our guide even unto death.

Philippians 4:13

I can do all things through Christ which strengtheneth me.

The Prime Directive

One day I was in a Christian bookstore and realized that most of the material they had to offer was on how to prepare yourself for the return of Christ or how America is going down the tubes morally and financially. Those topics are certainly of great importance, but in the back of my mind, I couldn't help but wonder if those books were on the shelf only because books with "End of Times" themes are big sellers and money makers. Christ told us that we would not be able to predict his return. So many people are so busy looking for the return of Christ that it seems as though they are forgetting that there is still work to be done in this world.

One common phrase we often hear is that "we are in this world, but we are not of this world." This reminds me of a television show I used to watch called "Star Trek." Most of you have probably heard of this science fiction series on outer-space exploration. Their mission was to explore other worlds and the life in those worlds. Many times throughout the series, you would hear the cry of the Starship's Captain Kirk or Mr. Spock saying, "We must remember the Prime Directive." Their Prime Directive was to never alter the lives of the people in the worlds they explored. The Prime Directive was the single most important instruction issued for them to follow as they embarked upon their mission.

We have a mission of our own that God wants us to embark upon. Our mission is to win souls for God. We also have our own Prime Directive, which Christ gave to us in Mark 16:15: "Go ye into all the world, and preach the gospel to every creature." It is imperative that we pursue the completion of this commandment. I look around at this world and can't help but remember the words of Christ in Matthew 9:37: "The harvest truly is plenteous, but the laborers are few." I would like to encourage each and every one of you reading this book to keep pressing onward in Christ. I would also like to challenge all of you to seek God's face and pray for his will to be done through your life. Through Christ we have the power to see our dreams become a reality, but it all starts with us. We must first put our plans behind us and realize that God's plans take priority over ours. Go ahead! Dare to be different! Let God direct your life and he will make you happier than you ever would have imagined you could be in life!

Philippians 3:13, 14

Brethren, I count not myself to have apprehended: but this one thing I do, forgetting those things which are behind, and reaching forth unto those things which are before, I press toward the mark for the prize of the high calling of God in Christ Jesus.

Acts 26:16–18

But rise, and stand upon thy feet: for I have appeared unto thee for this purpose, to make thee a minister and a witness both of these things which thou hast seen, and of those things in the which I will appear unto thee; Delivering thee from the people, and from the Gentiles, unto whom now I send thee, To open their eyes, and to turn them from darkness to light, and from the power of Satan unto God, that they may receive forgiveness of sins, and inheritance among them which are sanctified by faith that is in me.

Hebrews 12:1, 2

Wherefore seeing we also are compassed about with so great a cloud of witnesses, let us lay aside every weight, and the sin which doth so easily beset us, and let us run with patience the race that is set before us, Looking unto Jesus the author and finisher of our faith; who for the joy that was set before him endured the cross, despising the shame, and is set down at the right hand of the throne of God.

2 Timothy 4:1–5

I charge thee therefore before God, and the Lord Jesus Christ, who shall judge the quick and the dead at his appearing and his kingdom; Preach the word; be instant in season, out of season; reprove, rebuke, exhort with all longsuffering and doctrine. For the time will come when they will not endure sound doctrine; but after their own lusts shall they heap to themselves teachers, having itching ears; And they shall turn away their ears from the truth, and shall be turned unto fables. But watch thou in all things, endure afflictions, do the work of an evangelist, make full proof of thy ministry.

Matthew 28:19, 20

Go ye therefore, and teach all nations, baptizing them in the name of the Father, and of the Son, and of the Holy Ghost: Teaching them to observe all things whatsoever I have commanded you: and, lo, I am with you always, even unto the end of the world. Amen.

Matthew 24:13, 14

But he that shall endure unto the end, the same shall be saved. And this gospel of the kingdom shall be preached in all the world for a witness unto all nations; and then shall the end come.

Ephesians 3:20, 21

Now unto him that is able to do exceeding abundantly above all that we ask or think, according to the power that worketh in us, Unto him be glory in the church by Christ Jesus throughout all ages, world without end. Amen.